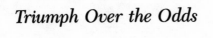
*Triumph Over the Odds*

# TRIUMPH
## *Over the Odds*

## Inspirational Success Stories

Louis Baldwin

A BIRCH LANE PRESS BOOK
*Published by Carol Publishing Group*

A Birch Lane Press Book
Published by Carol Publishing Group
Birch Lane Press is a registered trademark of Carol Communications, Inc.
Editorial Offices: 600 Madison Avenue, New York, N.Y. 10022
Sales & Distribution Offices: 120 Enterprise Avenue, Secaucus, N.J. 07094
In Canada: Canadian Manda Group, P.O. Box 920, Station U, Toronto,
    Ontario M8Z 5P9
Queries regarding rights and permissions should be addressed to
Carol Publishing Group, 600 Madison Avenue, New York, N.Y. 10022

Carol Publishing Group books are available at special discounts for bulk
purchases, sales promotions, fund-raising, or educational purposes.
Special editions can be created to specifications. For details, contact: Special
Sales Department, Carol Publishing Group, 120 Enterprise Avenue, Secaucus,
N.J. 07094

Manufactured in the United States of America
10  9  8  7  6  5  4  3  2  1


Library of Congress Cataloging-in-Publication Data

Baldwin, Louis.
    Triumph over the odds : inspirational success stories / Louis
Baldwin.
        p.   cm.
    "A Birch Lane Press book."
    ISBN 1-55972-238-X
    1. Celebrities— Biography.    2. Success.    I. Title.
CT105.B265   1994
920.02—dc20                                        94-20162
                                                        CIP

To Ginnie, with love.

# Contents

# Foreword

Words like *crushing* often precede the word *failure*, but failure isn't always what it's cracked up to be. It need not be the end of the world, even of one's own world. Sometimes, in a sense, it is only the beginning.

It has a long history of unexpected outcomes. The sketches offered here, spanning some thirty centuries, present many instances of turns of fate, triumphs over adversity, the snatching of success from the jaws of failure. They illustrate a quite common, and generally heartening, phenomenon.

# Moses and His Temper

As a young man Moses really, as we might put it today, had it made. He had everything going for him by every conventional measure of success in his time and place. But because of his temper, which he had not yet learned to control (especially in reacting to injustice), he lost it all. At the time the loss must have been devastating.

He was an Egyptian prince, accepted as the son of the Pharaoh's daughter. His Hebrew parents had left him as a baby on the banks of the Nile, at a place where he was likely to be found by the princess, because the Egyptian authorities were introducing infanticide as a method of population control among their Hebrew slaves. The parents' confidence in the princess's reputation for compassion proved justifiable: The baby was indeed found, and the princess understood immediately how he came to be there. And so, because she raised him as her son, he was a member of the royal family, in the line of succession. Honor, power, fame, wealth—already substantial—could only grow with time.

But perhaps blood is thicker than all such things. The young man seems to have been irresistibly attracted to the Hebrews, regularly watching them at their various labors. Also watching

1

them, of course, were Egyptian guards and supervisors, and one day about thirty-two centuries ago (the more remote the time, the less precise the dating), Moses saw an Egyptian in a secluded spot severely beating a Hebrew worker, and his gorge rose. He did have enough control of his temper to glance about in an effort to assure himself that they were unobserved, but not enough to keep him from attacking the Egyptian so violently that he killed him. Still unnoticed, and realizing that this was a capital offense even for (or perhaps especially for) a prince of the realm, he dug a pit, placed the body in it, and covered it with sand. He was confident that there had been no witnesses other than the Hebrew victim, who had fled the scene quite unceremoniously.

The next day, however, drained him of that confidence. This time he saw a Hebrew administering a beating to another Hebrew. Since the injustice in this case, if any, was not so clear, Moses merely held the aggressor immobile and asked why he was attacking a fellow Hebrew. Who are you, replied the man, to ask such a question? Who appointed you our judge? Do you intend to kill me now, as you killed the Egyptian yesterday? Moses relaxed his grip on the man as a wave of fear swept through him. So it was known—his murder of the Egyptian was so widely known that this fellow referred to it quite casually. Egypt had suddenly become a very dangerous place for the already fallen prince. The news of the murder surely had reached the Pharaoh by now, and his police must already be searching for the perpetrator. The situation clearly called for unhesitating emigration.

He left the country hastily. We do not know his route, and he surely had no particular destination, but according to the record he soon found himself in the country of Midian, on the eastern shore of the Red Sea. Trudging along through the bleak Sinai landscape, he came to a well, a small oasis. After slaking his desert thirst, he lay down to rest in the shade of a tree but was soon awakened by the music of women's voices at the well. He could see them from under the tree—there were seven of them—as they drew water from the well and poured it into the troughs for their family's sheep and goats to drink, and probably also into the large urns that they had brought with them for carrying water home in the traditional fashion of women in ancient cultures almost everywhere. And then, in the midst of their singing and chattering, he saw them look up in alarm. Their music was replaced by rougher sounds as several shepherds appeared on the scene, shouting at the women and driving them away from the well. Once again Moses found himself witnessing the brutality of the strong against the weak, and an irrepressible fury rose up within him. To the shepherds' astonishment he came at them out of the shadow of the tree like a rocket-propelled demon and fell upon the startled group like a mechanized flail, giving them a brief educational demonstration of how it feels to be on the receiving end. And they, unwilling to continue the course of instruction, dispersed precipitously.

The seven grateful maidens thereupon emerged from their spectators' haven and, with Moses' solicitous help, completed the watering of their animals and departed with greater dignity than the shepherds had been able to muster. But soon a few of them returned. Their father, they told Moses, was the chief priest (and perhaps, thereby, the political leader) of the Midianites. When he noticed that his daughters had come home from the well earlier than usual, he asked them why. They explained that the shepherds' customary amusement had been interrupted this time by a formidable traveler who had been resting at the well and who encouraged the interlopers to leave. Where is this man, he asked—still at the well? Yes, you *suppose* so? You mean you simply left him there, a weary and probably hungry traveler? Go back at once and bring him here, so that we can at least offer him a warm meal and some hospitality. And now, the daughters begged Moses, would he please come back with them and accept their father's invitation—and thereby smooth things over for them?

Moses, who doubtless had been moping over his isolation and bleak future, was delighted by this turn of events. He returned with the damsels and received a warm welcome from their father and other members of his extensive family—to which the father obviously thought he would make a splendid addition. Stay with us, he urged Moses, and I will give you my daughter Zipporah for a wife, and a flock of sheep and a herd of goats for you to tend. Whatever Moses may have thought of the offer, he had to compare it with the alternatives, which were virtually nonexistent. Further, he learned that the father was a worshiper not of many gods but of one, El (an old name for the Hebrews' God), and could thus be a source of information on the beliefs of those strange, dedicated people slaving away in bondage in his native land.

And so he stayed for nearly forty years. (There is a poignant significance in the fact that, when his son was born, he gave him a name meaning "stranger" or "foreigner.") The Pharaoh died and was replaced by another with no greater compassion for the children of Israel. News of this, and of the Hebrews' suffering under the Egyptian lash, must have reached Moses from time to time, but as the years passed and he settled into a fairly comfortable obscurity that before he would have found humiliating, events and conditions in Egypt must have seemed ever more distant and irrelevant. Besides, it was a Hebrew, after all, the very man whom he had rescued from a beating, who (he had every reason to think) had snitched on him. And, indeed, Moses had no reason to think that the Hebrews were particularly worth saving, even if it had occurred to him to do so.

The idea was forced on him, however. One day as he was tending the sheep he noticed a bush that was ostensibly on fire but, curiously, not being consumed by the flame. As he approached the burning bush, he heard a voice coming from it, calling his name. He responded, and the voice identified itself as that of the God of the Hebrews, who was about to rescue his people from the land of their oppression. And I want you, the voice informed the riveted Moses, to go to Egypt and tell the Pharaoh that you have come to lead the Hebrews away.

Moses was flabbergasted. *Me?* I'm nobody—how can I tell the Pharoah a thing like that?

You'll do it, the voice replied, because I will be with you.

But the Hebrews will ask who sent me—what can I tell them? What name can I give them?

Tell them that you have been sent by "I AM," the God of their ancestors, who will lead them to a rich, fertile country.

And so it went, with the voice insisting that Moses do as he was told, and Moses objecting that he had a speech impediment, that he was not persuasive enough to get the Hebrews to listen, and please, sir, send somebody else! But the voice won out in the end, and thereupon Moses, who had failed so miserably in the prince business, embarked on a career that would keep his name alive long after his name as a pharaoh would have been forgotten. The man who could not keep his temper would lead one of the most nettlesome, difficult groups of people in history through forty years of hardship and frustration, and he would do it without losing his temper (with one famous exception on Mount Sinai, in which commandments were broken both literally and figuratively). Under circumstances that would have had Job crawling up every available wall, he displayed incredible tolerance and patience. And although he was destined not to enter it himself, he did lead his people to the Promised Land.

# Cleopatra and the Gabinians

The name Cleopatra was a very common one in the ancient Mediterranean world. Alexander the Great had a sister named Cleopatra, and Plato mentions an earlier king of Macedonia with a wife by that name. Several Cleopatras can be found wandering about in the mythology of the region, and several more were Macedonian queens of Egypt. So many Cleopatras were there that the one whose reputation has survived over the past twenty centuries cannot be clearly identified by number—was she Cleopatra VI or Cleopatra VII?

Whatever her number, she was the Cleopatra who became queen in 51 B.C. at the age of eighteen, reigning in tandem with her ten-year-old brother Ptolemy, or with the regents acting for him during his minority. Her beauty may be more legendary than historical, especially in the eyes of remote beholders, but chroniclers of the period seem to agree on her attractiveness, even her seductiveness. She was indeed an enchantress, downright irresistible to two of the most famous leaders and sophisticated womanizers of her time, Julius Caesar and Marc Antony. She had a high intelligence, a forceful personality, and a well-honed ability to use her talents for getting her way. Coy she may have been at times,

6

for her purpose of the moment, but chronically demure she
certainly was not.

This may have been her undoing early in her career. Her dynasty
was Greek, imposed on native Egyptians by foreigners, at first by
Greeks and now by Romans. Indeed, her father, Auletes, who had
ruled as Ptolemy XII, had been deposed and forced to flee to Rome
for help because of native resentment as well as political intrigues in
the government of Alexandria. In Rome he had borrowed such a
huge sum from a Roman plutocrat that the latter's only hope of
repayment lay in restoring Auletes to the throne of Egypt. This had
been arranged by Aulus Gabinius, the governor of nearby Syria,
who led a contingent of mercenaries into Egypt and put Auletes
back in place, though to something less than popular acclaim.

To assure that Auletes would stay in power, Gabinius, on his
return to Syria, left behind a large number of his mercenaries,
troops mostly from Gaul and Germany. Over the next several years
these "Gabinians" became very Egyptian and indeed soon formed
a very influential nucleus of the Egyptian army. Cleopatra and
brother Ptolemy inherited them, and their support, after their
father died in 51 B.C. The new rulers could, of course, use any
support they could get, and, to get more, Cleopatra was wise
enough to court popularity by being the first in her line to learn to
speak Egyptian. In addition, she participated in Egyptian religious ceremonies, which had become fixed in Egyptian minds
and culture by centuries of adamantine tradition. Her participa-
tion was especially important because of the divinity the general
religious impulse of the people ascribed to royalty.

She may have carried these overtones farther than the Greek
ruling class in Alexandria could comfortably tolerate. There is a
record of her taking part in the installation of a new sacred bull at
the town of Hermonthis, several hundred miles south of Alexandria on the Nile. A shrine inscription there tells us that "the
queen, ... the goddess who loves her father ["Cleopatra" meant
"father-honorer"], rowed the Bull to Hermonthis in Amon's barge."
Although the actual rowing was a function of Egyptian manpower,

this sort of conspicuous cooperation with the Egyptians' worship of animals, which the Greeks found odious, must have pursed lips and pricked ulcers in the upper political echelons at Alexandria.

The anxiety in those classes was steadily sharpened by Cleopatra's persistent neglect of brother Ptolemy as comonarch. Rigid Egyptian tradition decreed that a woman could never rule alone, and even the strongest queens in the past had conformed, at least outwardly, to this restriction. Cleopatra, however, took a very dim view of sharing power with anyone, and especially with the regents acting for the boy, since they were her social inferiors and political subordinates. As a result, she exceeded her most forceful predecessors in asserting her royal prerogatives. The coins of her time, for example, bore her image alone, as though Ptolemy never existed; nothing so radical had ever been done before. In addition, she debased new coinage by reducing the coins' precious metal content and stamping a value on their face, thereby introducing a measure of inflation that the Greeks, as creditors, generally found excruciating. It was all very unsettling to the nervous regents, who with every passing day grew more eager to rid the kingdom of her and settle down with the much more manageable Ptolemy.

To add to the tension, Cleopatra soon after her accession managed to offend the anti-Roman sentiments of both Greeks *and* Egyptians and at the same time alienate the formidable Gabinian mercenaries. A new Roman governor of Syria named Bibulus, needing some help to defend his borders against a threat from Parthia to the east, was reminded that the Gabinians might be available. The Roman hopefully sent his two sons to hire as many Gabinians as they could (after touching base with Cleopatra) for service with the Syrian army. But the Gabinians showed little eagerness for leaving their homes to serve under a tough Roman general, and against the power of persuasion their refusal to serve became a stubborn one. We do not know what the sons of Bibulus did at this point, whether they grew intolerably importunate or otherwise offensive—they may have been afraid to go home empty-handed—but we do know that they were murdered.

Cleopatra, courageously or rashly or both, ordered the murderers arrested and shipped off to Bibulus for Roman justice. Her political adversaries could not have asked for a more golden opportunity, especially at a time when crop failures were aggravating tensions throughout the kingdom. Now, in the year 50 B.C., royal decrees began appearing with both Cleopatra's and Ptolemy's names, suggesting that the regents' power was waxing while hers was waning because of the widespread consternation over the surrender of the patriotic assassins. In the following year—the precise time is not clear—her position became so untenable that she had to leave Alexandria, escaping south to more friendly territory. Evidently pursued by vengeful Gabinians, she soon had to leave Egypt altogether, seeking refuge eventually in the independent coastal city-state of Ashkelon, in Palestine. She stayed there about a year. We have no information on how severely her morale was affected by her failure, except that in Lucan's *Pharsalia* (which may be more poetry than history) she is described as distraught.

Julius Caesar arrived in Alexandria in 48 B.C. Cleopatra's arrival shortly thereafter is colorfully depicted in George Bernard Shaw's *Caesar and Cleopatra:* It could well be true that she was smuggled into the city and his headquarters rolled up in a carpet. He was immediately and thoroughly captivated, and their love affair began at once, abetted no doubt by his excellent command of Greek. Her reign lasted for seventeen years. She survived Ptolemy XII, Ptolemy XIII, Ptolemy XIV, Caesar, and Marc Antony. But not the asp.

# Jesus and the Establishment

Jesus of Galilee was probably the most spectacularly successful abysmal failure in all history. Whether his success was only posthumous in the strictest sense may be a question more of faith than of history, but the contrast between the failure of his ideas to catch on during his lifetime and their subsequent widespread, durable popularity is too striking for his story to be omitted from a collection of this kind.

An irony in the contrast is that his ideas have survived in such rigidly institutionalized forms, through both Catholic and Protestant establishments. His ideas during his brief public life were considered thoroughly subversive, as indeed they were, and his few faithful followers were so unnerved by his radical teaching, and so loosely knit, that their immediate reaction to his arrest was to scatter like leaves in a storm. Early in his career the priestly political establishment paid little attention to him, distracted as it was by the radicalism of his friend and cousin John the Baptist. But after John was eliminated by Herod's grisly party (made so famous by the stimulating gyrations of the young Salome), the authorities became more aware of this other itinerant preacher who had created havoc among the money changers at the great temple in

Jerusalem and who continually treated questions from their fellow ecclesiastical pooh-bahs with amused disdain or withering scorn. Indeed, his responses were often quite personal, labeling highly respected dignitaries as serpents, spawn of the devil, hypocrites, and whitewashed tombs, clean looking on the outside but filthy within.

Of course he also said a great many other things, especially about loving God and one's neighbors, but the authorities were more interested in his canonical views—on washing cups properly, for instance, paying tithes precisely, fussing over rubrical niceties, and scrupulously avoiding any kind of work, even healing, on the Sabbath. Toward matters of this sort he showed an alarming indifference, even contempt, going so far as to assert the moral preeminence of acts of kindness over ceremonial sacrifices—and impudently quoting their own scriptures at them to prove his point. He further asserted the importance of personal humility and detachment from material possessions, adding, astonishingly, that a poor person ordinarily will rank higher in God's order than a rich one.

To this injury against their law and order he added the insult of an agile wit. On one occasion, as he finished talking to a crowd, they challenged him to tell them by what authority he acted. First you tell *me*, he replied, by what authority did John the Baptist act? The brighter ones among them immediately saw that he had given them a problem. They went into a huddle: If we say that John acted by God's authority, the crowd here will ask why we persecuted him, and if we say merely by his own authority, they will certainly start throwing things. And so they answered Jesus pusillanimously, We cannot tell you. Very well then, he shot back, neither will I tell you by what authority *I* act. And on another, more famous occasion they tried to trap him in a dilemma, asking him amid a crowd whether it was right for the Jewish people to pay Roman taxes. If he answered yes, they conjectured, he would lose the respect of his fellow Jews; and if he answered no, they could eagerly report him to the Roman procurator, Pontius Pilate, as a subversive. But he merely grinned and asked to see one of the coins with which the taxes were to be paid. A Roman coin was produced, he looked at it for a moment, and then he asked rhetorically whose image was stamped on it. Why, Caesar's, they answered uneasily. All right then, he responded, pay to Caesar whatever is Caesar's and to God whatever is God's. And presumably there was a considerable gnashing of teeth.

But this man was far more than an adroit debater. Reports of his healing activities were rife throughout the land. The lame, the blind, the diseased, together with those who only wanted to hear him speak, sometimes would press on him in such numbers that he would be forced to the edge of the Sea of Galilee and into a boat, from which he would speak to them while afloat. His cures were quite often spectacular (however easily we may think they can be explained today), impressive enough to give his opinions on love versus ritual great weight with the people. Indeed, a common opinion was that he spoke with genuine authority, in sharp contrast to the regulatory nitpickers who represented the establishment. The question of his authority became crucial as anxiety increased among the theocrats. Not only did he claim that his authority came directly from God and that he was God's special messenger, but he also kept hinting broadly that he had a unique relationship with God—that whereas all Jews were called sons of God, he was *the* Son of God. A raving lunatic from the establishment's viewpoint, a lunatic who lost many of his followers when he spoke of eating his flesh and drinking his blood, but a lunatic who could inspire multitudes, threatening the law and order, the very maintenance, of a properly run society. Small wonder that the establishment's chambers echoed with proposals for getting rid of him.

A golden opportunity arose in the third year of his public life, during the celebration of the Jewish feast of the Passover, commemorating the Jews' escape from Egypt some thirteen hundred years before. Jesus arrived in Jerusalem to a tumultuously friendly welcome from the festive crowds. The authorities hesitated to arrest him publicly because of his popularity, but their opportunity to do so more privately, at night, came to them in the form of his betrayer, Judas Iscariot, who, for a famous thirty pieces of silver, offered to lead them to him in a grove of olive trees where he had gone to pray. There they found him and arrested him and took him to the residence of the old priest Annas for questioning. But Jesus refused to answer the priest's questions (Jewish law did not require him to testify against himself), and his lack of servility in this kangaroo court so enraged one of the priest's retainers that the man struck the bound Jesus a severe blow. But Jesus responded mildly with a request that the evidence against him, if such there was, be formally presented.

To this end he was taken to the court of the High Priest Caiaphas, where a hastily assembled rump council was taking evidence from witnesses. The testimony was so contradictory, however, that Caiaphas finally turned to Jesus in desperation and almost begged him to say whether he was the Hebrews' long-awaited Messiah, the Son of God. That I am, replied Jesus, thereby coming close enough to blasphemy under Jewish law for Caiaphas to tear at his clothing in a ritualistic reaction to blasphemy and to demand a verdict from the council. They gave it to him forthwith, and unanimously: This miscreant deserves the death penalty. And they turned Jesus over for the rest of the night to the derisive mistreatment of his guards.

The next day he was hauled off to the headquarters of Pontius Pilate, since the death penalty required Roman approval. Pilate's role in the drama seems to have been that of a world-weary bureaucrat forced to give his time and attention to a local quarrel in which he had no interest and no stake except that, if allowed to get out of hand, it could bring him some unwelcome attention from Rome. He played his part warily, interrogating Jesus rather perfunctorily and, in the end, after an elaborate public disclaimer of any responsibility in the matter, turning him over to his soldiers for that ingeniously cruel and humiliating form of death, crucifixion.

Jesus hung on that tree of torture for several hours, derided by spectators and abandoned by nearly all his friends, until the hopelessness of his bitter destiny wrung from him the famous plaintive cry, "My God, my God, why have you forsaken me?" And indeed, who casually watching this scene would have thought it anything but the squalid end of one more insignificant troublemaker?

Troublemaker he was. But hardly insignificant.

# Muhammad and the Quraish of Mecca

In the year 619 Muhammad was nearly fifty years old. Ten years earlier he had received his first call to proclaim the uniqueness and absolute supremacy of Allāh, the one and only God. In all that time his followers had never numbered more than a few dozen. In his tribe, the Quraish of Mecca, and to a great extent even in his clan, the Beni Hāshim, he was as close to being an outcast as the Arabian extended-family concept of society allowed. His outlandish ideas threatened the thriving tourist business that had grown up around the Kaaba in Mecca, the great temple sacred to Abraham and Ishmael but now crowded with pagan idols. He was about as popular as Jesus had been among the money changers in Jerusalem.

He had survived chiefly because of two people. One was his devoted wife, Khadija, his first convert, who had given him the protection and support of her considerable wealth, energy, and love. The other was his uncle, Abu Talib, generally recognized as the leader of the Hashim clan. Although Abu Talib never accepted his nephew's teachings, he was impressed by his unwavering

15

conviction and dedication. One day he was visited by leaders of several other clans in the Quraish tribe who were heavily involved in Kaaba merchandising. They complained that Muhammad was preaching a doctrine against the validity of the Kaaba idols, and this was not good for business. Indeed, if generally accepted, it could ruin them. Further, he was preaching that those who rejected his teaching—past, present, and future—would be eternally damned by Allāh, and this meant that all their revered ancestors were roasting in the fires of hell. We've had him up to here, they told Abu Talib, and you had better shut him up, one way or another, or we will—and perhaps you as well.

Abu Talib summoned Muhammad, told him about the visit, and begged him to hold his tongue. Muhammad replied that he could not give up his vocation even if offered the sun and the moon to do so. He must go on until he won the world for Allāh or died in the attempt. He valued his uncle's protection, but what must be, must be. As he was about to leave, Abu Talib, deeply moved, called him back and promised always to protect him, whatever he might say.

And he did just that. On his deathbed in 619—shortly after Khadija's death—he received another, similar visit from the Meccan establishment to ask that he send for Muhammad and try to arrange some compromise that he and they could live with. When Muhammad arrived, however, the only compromise that he would countenance was for everyone to acknowledge openly, "There is no God but Allāh and Muhammad is His Messenger." The Quraish leaders, finding this less than conciliatory, refused to negotiate further. Abu Talib died without accepting Islam, which means subjection to the will of God, and therefore presumably went to hell.

Deciding that Mecca might soon prove uncomfortable, Muhammad shortly left for a village about fifty miles to the southeast. There he was granted an interview with the village leaders, whom he immediately tried to convert. They reacted with derision: If God really needs a messenger, can't he find anything better than you? In fact, they added, if you really are God's messenger, you're too exalted a creature for us to deal with you. If you're not, you're too lowly a creature for us to deal with you. His claims quickly spread through the village, and soon a crowd appeared well armed with stones, those universally popular instruments for chastening mavericks. He fled the village and took refuge in a local vineyard, where he was hidden by the compassionate owners.

Although safe for the moment, he could hardly expect to spend the rest of his life in a vineyard. Wary of going back to Mecca without any protection, he sent messages to several chieftains in the neighborhood, asking for protection on his return to the city. Although all were idolaters, one did offer protection, apparently on condition that Muhammad quit his preaching. But on his return Muhammad found that even his own clan, now headed by a hostile successor of Abu Talib, had turned against him. He was very much alone, forced to limit his preaching to unsympathetic Bedouins who camped from time to time about the city. His only consolation seems to have been that the Quraish now generally did not bother him, apparently considering his influence too insignificant to merit their attention. Yet he surely knew that any serious resumption of his preaching would reinvigorate them.

One day in 620, as he was making his rounds of the visitors' camps, he fell into conversation with a group of seven pilgrims from the oasis town of Yathrib, about 250 miles north of Mecca. Yathrib boasted five small tribes, three of which were Jewish in their religious beliefs, the other two idolatrous. These seven pilgrims were idolaters, but they knew that their Jewish neighbors expected a messiah, and Muhammad sounded to them like a prime candidate. They promised to give his claims some serious consideration during the coming year.

That year seems to have been Muhammad's most depressing. All of Islam consisted only of him and his tiny, scattered band of converts. Stony indifference, ridicule, frustration were his daily fare. Small wonder that he looked forward to the return of the Yathrib pilgrims, who seemed his only, slender hope. And they proved as good as their word. This time they brought five more men with them, and in the mountains outside Mecca they made the pledge, promising Muhammad to worship only Allāh, renouncing thievery, fornication, infanticide, and slander, and pledging obedience to God's Messenger in all that was right. In return, Muhammad promised a posthumous welcome into Paradise. When they went back to Yathrib, one of Muhammad's few Meccan converts accompanied them.

In 622 the new Yathrib Moslems arrived at Mecca with a large group of idolatrous pilgrims. After the pagan ceremonies at the Kaaba the faithful dozen or so returned at night to the place in the mountains where they had gathered before. After Muhammad joined them, they came to an agreement with him. If he would come to Yathrib with them as a resident, they would protect him, by force if necessary, from any adversaries. Any followers of his now in Mecca also would be welcome. Muhammad, having recently received a revelation approving the use of force by Moslems in defending their rights, accepted their offer.

After filing past him and striking his hand as a pledge of their good faith, the Yathribis returned to their caravan and melted in among their sleeping companions.

The next morning some Quraish chiefs got wind of what was going on. Suddenly they were anxious to detain Muhammad now that he was thinking of leaving. They accused the caravan leaders of engaging in a conspiracy with him, but of course the infidels had no idea of what they were talking about, and the Quraish effort proved abortive. When the Moslems arrived in Yathrib they were well received and even given a place to settle at the south end of the oasis.

But Muhammad was not yet with them. He had stayed behind, perhaps in the hope of negotiating the release of a few Moslems who were being held back by their families. A council of Quraish leaders meanwhile concluded that the only solution to their new problem—they feared that Muhammad with his gathering strength in Yathrib might be far more dangerous to them than he had been even in Mecca—was simply to kill the prophet in his own country, or city. To avoid individual responsibility falling on any single clan, they agreed on a Caesarean type of assassination, with one man from each clan thrusting a dagger into the victim. But their plot was foiled by their own lack of organization and leaky secrecy. Muhammad was brought word and escaped with a disciple to a cave some three miles south of town (rather than north, toward Yathrib). There they remained in hiding for the next three days.

Their journey to Yathrib was rugged, since they felt that the regular caravan route would be too risky. Nevertheless on a summer day in 622, they surmounted a ridge and there before them lay the inviting green oasis. The Yathrib Moslems, who had been anxiously awaiting news of them, ran out to greet them— "He has come! He has come!" For the next three or four days, in a small settlement by the town, the weary prophet rested among his friends.

On the fourth or fifth day he mounted a camel and rode into Yathrib. Along the way he received many offers from families to stay with them, but he answered that he had determined to stay on the camel until Allāh ordered the animal to stop. It did so in front of a barn used to store dates. A young man came out from an adjoining house and asked Muhammad to stay with him and his family. Muhammad agreed, and the young Moslim took his baggage into the house. Who, asked the prophet, owns the barn? He was told and, after buying it from the owner with some money offered by a disciple, asked that work to renovate it be started immediately. It was to be the world's first mosque. And thenceforward Yathrib was to be known as Medina.

# Alfred the Great and the Battle of Chippenham

In the late 860s Alfred of Wessex, although still in his teens, was already an experienced soldier.

For more than a generation England had been suffering the Viking scourge. The Danish Vikings especially had made themselves aggressively at home through the eastern half and the midsection of the island, including some of the bellied peninsula now called Wales.

These amphibious nomads were the terror of Europe. Using the rivers as military highways, the fierce, ruthless Danish pirates pillaged town after town, sacking Paris twice, plundering Seville, even defeating the Moors in Morocco. Their raids on the eastern shores of England, beginning a little before the year 800, were at first occasional, then more frequent but sporadic, and always devastating. The raiders particularly enjoyed visiting the country's monasteries, which offered them large quantities of precious metals and gems for easy appropriation and large numbers of monks for instant martyrdom. Indeed, the lure of other monasteries farther inland may have been the chief reason for their decision to accelerate their casual raiding into an all-out effort at conquest. In 865 a fleet of hundreds of ships landed a large army on England's east coast, and within four years the Danes had conquered or essentially subdued five of England's Anglo-Saxon kingdoms. Only Wessex, occupying the southwest portion of the island, remained intact. And formidably surrounded.

Young Alfred was increasingly involved as time passed and the Danes grew ever more threatening. His father, King Ethelwulf of Wessex, and his three elder brothers spent much of their time leading bands of part-time warriors in largely futile efforts to help Saxon defenders in the surrounding kingdoms. Alfred, despite a deep-seated preference for books over swords, found himself accompanying them more and more often. By the end of the decade he was second in command; he and his brother King Ethelred were the family's sole male survivors.

Ethelred was a man of rather stubborn piety. On a chilly morning in January 871 he was in his tent, hearing mass, while Alfred waited impatiently on a battlefield where Saxon and Viking warriors were facing each other and engaging in the customary preliminaries of mutual reassurance and menacing bravado. To a messenger sent to remind him of his secular responsibilities, Ethelred replied curtly that the mass wasn't over yet, that he would not "leave divine service for the service of men." On the battlefield, however, the Danes were showing signs that they might not care to wait. Alfred observed their noisy impatience with growing alarm. He and his rustic warriors were going to have to fight uphill as it was, and he was not disposed to give the enemy the added advantage of making the first move.

And so *he* made it. As the Danes closed up their wall of shields— a move that generally preceded an attack—Alfred passed the order to his Saxons to do the same and then, with a loud shout, sprang forward "like a wild boar," as a chronicler of the battle put it. By the time Ethelred arrived from his devotions, the two armies were joined and intermingled in noisy, lethal fray. After untold hours of bloody melee, the Danes decided that their path of least resistance lay to the east and hastily took French leave in that direction. The surviving Saxons evidently were too exhausted to think of giving chase. This was the battle of Ashdown, and the Danes did not stop running until they arrived at Reading, some twenty miles away.

The battle was by no means decisive. Although it revealed something of Alfred's military mettle and talent for leadership, its effect on the Danes was minimal. In less than a fortnight they were conducting hit-and-run raids out of Reading and even had established a garrison to the southwest, perhaps thirty miles into Wessex territory. King Ethelred and Alfred led an assault on this camp, but it proved too much for them. They retired to count their losses, forced to content themselves with the hope that at least they had stopped the Danes from penetrating even deeper into their land.

They had a problem like the one faced by George Washington nine centuries later. The Danish forces consisted of fulltime fighters, but the Saxon troops were primarily farmers, mixed with a few artisans, peddlers, etc., who had to be persuaded by the Wessex leaders to leave their plows and tools long enough to do some fighting. Although they had plenty of incentive to protect their families and their property and fought lustily when the occasion demanded, they tended to melt back into the landscape after a battle, so that a disproportionate amount of time and energy had to be devoted to recruitment between engagements.

This problem may have been a major factor in the next important battle. After the battle of Ashdown in January, it seems, the Saxon army largely drained away into the Wessex farms and towns. In late March Ethelred and Alfred led such troops as they had in an attack on the Danish salient. After much fierce fighting, the Danes retreated, but only to return in a counterattack that brought them victory. The record of the battle is unclear; the Saxons evidently became disheartened toward evening, perhaps because King Ethelred was wounded seriously and had to quit the field.

He died in mid-April, leaving two small sons too young for the throne and a brother able, though not very willing, to occupy it. Alfred's reluctance was not lessened by the news from the east that countless Danish reinforcements had landed on the coast and were already camped at Reading, eagerly awaiting an opportunity to drive the Wessex defenders into the sea. He may have lacked enthusiasm also because of the earlier fate of King Edmund of East Anglia, whom the Danes reportedly executed by tying him to a stake and using him as a target for archery practice.

Nevertheless, recognizing the lack of honorable alternatives, he accepted his royal responsibilities. Fortunately, the Danes' eagerness for battle may have been overestimated, or at least now overruled by a growing anxiety to consolidate their conquests of the other kingdoms. While they were thus distracted, Alfred managed to survive the rest of the year 871, and in the winter used their new preoccupation to trade them ransom money for a promise to leave Wessex in peace. He knew, of course, that the promised peace could be no more than a temporary truce, perhaps no more than a short reprieve.

But it lasted five years. For Alfred, five busy years. He was sure that the Danes would be back, and the warmth of their welcome on that occasion was his responsibility. He traveled incessantly about his little kingdom, organizing a reserve militia that could, he hoped, respond quickly and reliably to any Danish incursions. In some of the coastal towns he started the rudiments of an English navy to counteract the Danes' advantage at sea. As reports of his feverish activity reached the Danes, they began to suspect that he might turn out to be the one person in the known world able and willing to resist the Viking hordes. And so they decided to do something about him.

In the spring of 876 they invaded Wessex with a large force, cutting a swath of ruthless pillage to the southern coast, where they set up a garrison by the sea. Alfred responded by issuing a call to arms and laying siege to the intruders' camp. Although the camp could be supplied by sea and therefore could not be starved into surrender, Alfred counted on Danish wanderlust to make their impoundment intolerable. He counted right. By summer the Danes were stir-crazy enough to ask for a truce—and for more money as the price of their leaving Wessex altogether. Alfred agreed and withdrew his forces enough to permit their departure. But the Danes, breaking their word, rushed out of the camp, attacked the Saxons to throw them off balance, and headed north. Alfred and company quickly recovered, overtook the Danes, forced them back into their camp, and renewed the siege. As winter approached, the Danes, exhausted mentally and physically by their confinement and discouraged by the loss of over a hundred ships and thousands of reinforcements in a heavy autumn storm, gave up. Offering Alfred hostages against any repetition of their previous deception, they agreed to leave Wessex peacefully. And leave they did, to the astonishment of all, probably including themselves.

This time the respite lasted only about a year. In the winter of 877–78 another large force, led by the Danish king Guthrum, swept into Wessex and established a garrison in an easily defensible river location at Chippenham, about fifty miles due west of Ashdown. While they used this position as a base for raids in various southerly directions, a Danish fleet attacked the southern shore of the Wessex peninsula. This pincer assault led to a battle so fierce and unexpected that the Saxons succumbed. Many of the kingdom's leaders even left precipitously for France.

But not Alfred. With a few retainers he retreated to the forests and fens near the northern shore of the Wessex peninsula, hiding there, according to one chronicler, "in great sorrow and unrest amid the woods and marshes of the land of Somerset." He was now nearly thirty years old. He had spent his whole adult life, ten grueling years, planning and organizing and fighting in his unremitting struggle to force the Danes to leave his land and his people alone. And now that long, bitter struggle had ended in utter defeat, in total failure. He was a beaten man.

His low spirits, and low status, appear in a now famous tale that he enjoyed telling in his later years. One day shortly after the defeat at Chippenham he took a walk through the woods, wearing rough peasant clothing as a protective disguise. Coming upon a cowherd's hut, he asked the peasant woman there to let him rest a while by the fire. She replied that he could do so if he would watch her cakes and turn them to keep them from burning. Alfred agreed but was soon absorbed in thought. He was startled from his reverie when the woman, summoned by the odor of burning cakes, rushed in to rescue them and then loudly threatened him ("You sot!") with a whack on the nose for his neglect. To this favor, as Hamlet might put it, had the king of Wessex come. He could not laugh at that until much later.

But his experience is instructive. Patience in adversity not only softens the adversity but, more important, offers time for spiritual, or psychological, recovery. Black Tuesday rarely looks so black on Wednesday. Before long Alfred rebounded and began thinking of possible ways out of the depths. Soon he was sending emissaries throughout Wessex to rally the Saxon warriors into a state of militant readiness. Encouraged by their response, he devised a plan and dispatched messengers with instructions for assembling at a secret rendezvous not far from Chippenham. There, in the spring of 878, he joined his irrepressible battlers and began marching toward the Danish camp. The Danes met them south of Chippenham, near present-day Edington. The Saxons attacked without ceremony and, after hours of hewing and smiting, broke up the Danish formations and chased the enemy north back to Chippenham. This was a distance of fourteen miles, but Alfred and his Saxons proved not only irrepressible but also inexhaustible. During the chase they slew thousands of the invaders and took possession of great amounts of supplies. Arriving at the garrison, they immediately lay siege to it, and this time their adversaries had no outlet to the sea. Within a couple of weeks the hungry, restless Danes unconditionally surrendered.

Alfred took the occasion of his victory to show that he could be patient in others' adversity as well as in his own. Far from leaping at the opportunity for sweet revenge, he opted for sweet charity, providing the Danes with food and clothing and such medical care as he could. His treatment impressed them enough to persuade the pagan Guthrum to become a Christian, the first Dane to do so but by no means the last. Since England was not overpopulated, there was room for Danes and Saxons to live together on the island in peace. Under Alfred's direction, they learned to do so, by and large. They separated, with Danes predominating in the east and Saxons in the west. Some hostility remained, of course, but without hostilities. And Alfred, although partly occupied with building up England's defenses against future Viking invasions, could now indulge his love of learning. It was surely for this love, and not for any love of battle, that he became known, uniquely among British monarchs, as "the Great."

# Galileo and the Inquisition

In 1638 John Milton visited Italy, where he found intellectuals in a state of chronic depression over "the servile condition into which learning amongst them was brought." He was saddened and angered at the sight of an outstanding victim of that condition in Florence. "There it was that I found and visited the famous Galileo, grown old, a prisoner of the Inquisition for thinking in Astronomy other than the Franciscan and Dominican licensers of thought."

Galileo Galilei lived precariously because of a risky combination of an independent mind, a gift for ridicule, and, consequently, a vast and varied collection of resentful enemies. As an independent thinker, he had no patience with the appeals to authority characteristic of the polemics of his time and place. In 1623, for example, in an extended controversy over the nature and temperature of comets, his adversary appealed to the authority of a Greek historian's report that Babylonian soldiers, when unable to light fires, cooked their eggs by whirling them around in slings. Galileo replied by reporting an experiment: He had hired some athletic Italians to whirl raw eggs around in slings. Not only did the process fail to cook the eggs, but it actually cooled off heated eggs.

Therefore, Galileo explained, since the only difference between the two incidents was the nationality of the participants, his adversary must be saying that the eggs were cooked because the whirlers were Babylonian. Such verbal demolitions naturally tended to win more debates than influential friends.

This contempt for dim-witted trust in authority was chronic, as much a part of Galileo's character as his passion for scientific demonstration. It surfaced quite visibly in a letter he wrote to the astronomer Johannes Kepler in 1597, when he was in his early thirties. He had much earlier been converted to the Copernican hypothesis of the earth and the other planets orbiting the sun, he confided, but had been afraid to publish any such opinion lest his work be denounced like that of Copernicus, "who, although he achieved everlasting fame among a few, among the many is mocked and jeered at, so great is the number of fools." Although the fools were not such great fools (nor perhaps as numerous) as Galileo supposed, they did have a very human tendency to resist any fact that collided with authoritative opinion—especially, for them, the opinion of the reverend Aristotle as extrapolated by the similarly reverend St. Thomas Aquinas. Human observation of the universe must conform to the orthodox interpretation of God's scripture and "the natural law" or—and here lay the deadly foolishness—be forcibly suppressed. Aristotle himself would have been appalled.

Galileo struggled against this kind of presumption throughout his professional life, trying to save his church from the prideful ignorance of its leadership. His unique reports on his observations through his telescopes—on the irregularity of the moon's surface, the spots on the sun, the phases of Venus, the moons of Jupiter, the protuberances (rings) of Saturn, the discrete stars in the Milky Way—were such models of gracefully written exposition that they won him an impressive audience among European intellectuals. It was much too impressive for the comfort of the academics whose reputations and livelihoods rested on Ptolemy's stationary earth orbited by the universe—one of whom actually refused to look through a telescope on the grounds that God must not approve such observation, or He would have given mankind innate telescopic vision. Since most of these scholarly name droppers were clerics—Milton's Franciscans and Dominicans but also many Jesuits—their chief line of attack naturally became one of ecclesiastical mischief making. Dominican preachers reported Galileo to the Inquisition as a disseminator of blasphemy, since he was suggesting that the earth and its contents might consist of the same kind of matter as the rest of the universe (a serious no-no in St. Thomas's cosmology); moreover, as a Copernican, he declined to believe that the earth and mankind represented the focal point about which the universe turned.

Galileo grew ever more anxious not so much over his own fate as over the fate of his church. His perennial hope and ambition was to reconcile the burgeoning accumulation of new scientific data with the dominant theological opinions of his day. Desperately he wrote to authorities in Rome begging for more openness of mind, pointing out precedents for interpreting scriptures allegorically rather than literally, and warning of the danger of injuring the church's credibility in making irrevocable pronouncements. He was not without support at the Vatican, but the most prominent theologian at the time was the Jesuit Cardinal Roberto Bellarmine, who had the last word.

The last thing Bellarmine wanted was a controversy that might hamper Rome's struggle against the Reformation, especially when the argument concerned nothing more than an inconsequential knowledge of mere physical reality. Further, the knowledge in question was that obtained through human observation and experiment rather than from the Bible, and who could deny that Solomon was divinely inspired when he spoke of the sun rising and setting and returning to its place? And so under the cardinal's aegis the Copernican view was condemned as false. In a personal audience he warned Galileo that he must not accept nor defend that view as true, although he would be permitted to discuss it merely as a hypothesis, a conjecture.

Galileo returned to Florence and continued his studies without any noticeable interference. In 1624, three years after Bellarmine's death, he traveled to Rome in the hope of getting the cardinal's order rescinded—a hope nourished by the fact that the new pope, Urban VIII, had been a friend and supporter before his election. It was a fateful visit. Partly because Galileo argued weakly that the existence of the tides proves that the earth moves, he did not obtain a reversal of the Bellarmine edict, but the pope did give him permission to publish a book on the two major "systems of the world," the Ptolemaic and the Copernican, as long as the book remained noncommittal and did not denigrate the omnipotence of God by suggesting restrictions on His choice of methods of running the world. Galileo again returned to Florence, where he spent the next eight years preparing his most celebrated work, *A Dialogue on the Two Major World Systems*. It was published in 1632, complete with an imprimatur from a friendly censor who lived to regret it, and was hailed throughout Europe as a masterpiece.

It was so hailed, of course, by those who shared Galileo's impatience with Aristotelian dogma. Despite the papal injunction against its making any commitment to either "system," the *Dialogue* was readily interpreted by Copernicans as a defense of their viewpoint. A major reason for this was that Galileo, partly to avoid any conspicuous commitment, resorted to one of his favorite literary tools, irony, which takes on meaning chiefly in the eye of the beholder. In the book, for instance, he has Simplicio, the Aristotelian, praise deduction based on authority over induction based on observation. Students, says Simplicio, "without being subjected to the rigors of inclement weather, may accumulate a thorough knowledge of nature simply by turning over a few pages." While Copernicans savored such dollops of acid, Aristotelians gagged.

Among those gagging was Pope Urban, who felt betrayed. Not only had Galileo disobeyed his order against taking sides, however thick the overlay of irony, but he had also put into the mouth of the dullard Simplicio some of the very arguments that Urban had advanced in his discussions with the astronomer. (Galileo evidently had not intended any such derisive implication, but such are the hazards of irony.) The anti-Galileans around Urban fanned these flames of resentment into a roaring fire, and in the fall of 1632 Galileo was ordered to come to Rome without delay and appear before the Inquisition. The order so shocked him that his health, never better than precarious, went into a precipitous decline. Despite certificates from three doctors warning that a trip to Rome at this time would imperil his life, the best he could get from the Vatican was a delay until December, after which he would be brought to the Holy City in chains. In January 1633, still ill and weak, he made the grueling twenty-three-day trip, arriving in mid-February. He could have easily escaped the papal reach in Switzerland or Venice, but he was still a loyal Catholic and, at least between bouts of depression, he believed stoutly that he would be vindicated.

He had reason to believe so. He and his friends felt that he had obeyed the letter if not the spirit of Urban's injunction. He had permission to present the Copernican system as a conjecture, and that, at least technically, was what he had done. He and his supporters probably were unaware of the depth of Urban's fury, and they clearly were unaware that the record now included an unsigned document, of highly suspicious origin, stating that in 1616 the Holy Office had ordered Galileo to "relinquish utterly" the idea of the earth's moving around the sun and never to defend it "in any way whatsoever, orally or in writing." Since this wording forbade defending it even as a conjecture, and since the document was to be introduced at the trial without warning, the inquisitors could already sniff the sweet smell of success.

Against such tactics Galileo, now seventy and ill, was helpless. At the trial that April all that he had with which to counter the inventive documentary evidence was his own testimony, based on dim recollections of events almost twenty years past, and an ambiguous letter from the now-deceased Cardinal Bellarmine.

Recognizing total defeat when he saw it, he confessed to mistakes of "ignorance and inadvertence" in the *Dialogue*, due to "vainglorious ambition." He might have remained unsubmissive, but he recognized that the controversy was not one of solid black versus solid white. Nor was he of an age or in a condition to face the torture that was the threatened alternative. And he was *still* a Roman Catholic.

His final hearing, in June, concerned not what he had written but what he believed. He testified that he had considered the Copernican view false since 1616. He and apparently everyone else at the hearing knew this assertion to be quite untrue, but by now the trial had worn itself down to a formality. He was sentenced to life imprisonment, copies of the *Dialogue* were ordered burned, his works were placed on the Index, and the pronouncement of the sentence, with its clear condemnation of any suggestion that the earth might move as contrary to scripture, was required to be read in all university communities.

Galileo's shocked dejection was profound. His long-held hope had been to bring the official church around to some recognition that literal interpretations of scripture were not the wells from which to draw information on the nature and history of the physical universe. He saw no contradiction between scientific facts and religious beliefs, and he had hoped to be the catalyst for their peaceful reconciliation. But he had failed in this ambition, miserably. "Who can doubt," he wrote bitterly, "that the worst disorders will result when minds made free by God are focused to submit slavishly to another will? When we are ordered to deny our senses and surrender them to the caprice of others? When people of any degree of incompetence are appointed judges over experts and given the authority to treat them as they like?"

Urban relented a bit, and the sentence was commuted to house arrest, though still for life. Galileo was first relegated to the custody of an old friend, the archbishop of Sienna, and then sent home to his villa near Florence. With the archbishop's encouragement he began to work again, not in astronomy but in less controversial areas of physics and mechanics. By and large, he spent the remaining eight years of his life in productive activity and some measure of content. The disappointment dimmed, although it could never fade completely.

In the autumn of 1980 Pope John Paul II ordered that the case be reopened to determine whether the decision at the trial ought to be formally reversed.

# George Washington and Fort Necessity

$B$etween 1756 and 1763 the Seven Years' War brought about major shifts in the incessant power struggles that constituted Europe's perennial and most devastating plague. More importantly, according to Prussia's Frederick the Great, who played a starring role, it took the lives of more than a million people, both soldiers and civilians. Its causes, such as royal greed and colonial ambition seasoned with popular chauvinism, had festered for generations, and by the middle of the eighteenth century Europe was ripe for an incident to set it off, for a trigger to be pulled. That trigger was pulled in the North American wilderness in May 1754 at the command of Lieutenant Colonel George Washington of the Virginia militia. Washington's command eventually, as Voltaire wrote later, "set Europe ablaze." It also set off a chain of events that did nothing to enhance the young officer's reputation.

He was under instructions to avoid firing the first shot in any engagement if at all possible. England and France were officially at peace and preferred to keep it that way, despite their spirited rivalry in the Ohio valley. In connection with this rivalry the

34

acting governor of Virginia, Robert Dinwiddie, had commissioned Washington in Alexandria to lead a band of about 150 men 200 miles into the wilderness and to garrison a strategic point at the site of modern Pittsburgh, thereby preventing the French from doing so. On the way there, however, Washington learned that the French had already occupied the area with a force much larger than his and had built a fort, Fort Duquesne, to defend it. Yet he continued to advance, cutting a primitive road through the mountain forests toward an Ohio Company storehouse that he could fortify while awaiting further orders and, he hoped, reinforcements.

He never made it to the storehouse. Friendly Indians reported that a French party was advancing toward him. In some alarm he decided to set up a makeshift fort in a large field about forty miles south of Fort Duquesne, which he described in a report as "a charming field for an encounter," although the "fort"—consisting essentially of nothing more than a square formed by trenches and wagons, to be aptly christened Fort Necessity—stood in the center, invitingly open to attack on all sides. One of the Indian chiefs described the fort contemptuously as "that little thing in the meadow" and urged Washington to move to a site with better natural defenses. But the young colonel remained adamantly charmed.

In addition, he was distracted by a report from a wandering frontiersman that a band of about fifty Frenchmen were not far away, and by a confirming Indian report that put the number nearer thirty. He set out at once with about forty men to join the dozen warriors who had sent him the report. The next morning, after discovering the French encamped in a hollow, his party and the Indians stealthily surrounded them. Stealthily, that is, until he unexpectedly found himself on a ridge in full view of the French. Having been discovered and seeing the French running for their muskets, he gave the fateful order to commence firing.

The French returned the fire, concentrating on Washington's exposed group rather than trying to return the fire of the more intelligently concealed Indians stationed on the opposite ridge. This first experience with the whine of so many bullets appealed to the readily enchantable Washington, who later wrote one of his brothers that he found "something charming in the sound." But the spell was soon over. Since the French camp was in a strategically naive position, even more vulnerable than that of Fort Necessity, the skirmish lasted only a quarter of an hour. The surviving French dropped their muskets and rushed to mingle with the Virginia riflemen for protection from the scalping that the Indians had already begun on the dead and wounded. Amid the uproar several of the French officers showed signs of righteous indignation. One, after pulling some papers from a pouch, flourished them at Washington with very angry gestures and very angry, though unintelligible, words.

Before long, with the help of three or four competitively incompetent interpreters, Washington learned that ten of the French had been killed and twenty-two had surrendered. Among the dead was their captain. The papers being presented so furiously were his credentials, which identified him as a diplomat rather than a soldier, an ambassador under instructions to find the English and offer to maintain the existing peace, but to warn them not to trespass on French territory. Washington considered these instructions simply "insolent," stoutly maintaining in his report to Dinwiddie that if the French had been on a peaceful mission they surely would have approached him more openly. His view of the incident, however, was to prove a minority opinion. Although he had defenders in the colony, the majority judgment, especially in the more exalted official quarters, was that he had precipitated what is now called the French and Indian war, the American precursor and prime cause of the Seven Years' War—despite Dinwiddie's attempt, in his report to London, to blame it all on the Indians.

On his return to Fort Necessity Washington, expecting a retaliatory visit from the French, directed his militiamen in building a wall of vertical posts around the area to provide "a small palisaded fort." Inside it, he reported, his small troop could withstand an attack from a force three times its size, although his sardonic Indian ally argued that the palisade would prove a trifling defense against an attack of seasoned, properly equipped soldiers. Washington's optimism was strengthened by the news that he had been promoted to full colonel by the bureaucratic mills and that reinforcements of some 300 men would soon join him. A third of these, when they arrived, turned out to be British regulars, beside whom the easygoing American frontiersmen looked downright slovenly. This royal company served under the command of a Scottish captain, McKay, who, having received his commission from the Crown, expected but failed to receive the deference he thought due him from the American colonel. He proved to be a practical, competent officer, however, who soon earned Washington's respect, and the two men learned to cooperate.

The cooperation did not extend to manual labor because the captain was not authorized to increase his soldiers' pay, as was required by regulations for such demeaning duty. When Washington led his men out to resume work on the hoped-for road, therefore, the British stayed comfortably in the fort (comfort being a very relative thing). And when he and his men returned with news that a force of 800 French and 400 Indians was on their trail, it was the Americans who added to the fortifications while the British watched, planting one more acorn for a tree of liberty. But at least they stayed. The Indians, thoroughly disgusted with what they considered Washington's paternalistic arrogance and stupidity, left the clearing for the greater security of the surrounding woods. Although Indians were, as Washington once wrote, "the best people in the world to improve a victory," they had little interest in displaying unrestrained heroism in white men's squabbles.

On the morning of July 3, 1754, the French broke into the clearing, evidently to their surprise, as though they had come upon it unexpectedly. Washington ordered his modest artillery (nine small swivel guns) to fire and then followed up with his musketry, and the enemy retreated hastily back into the forest. Now Washington would have his fill of that charming sound.

From the unseen enemy came a hail of lead that quickly drove the artillerymen from their guns and cut down the riflemen by the dozens, driving the survivors from one desperate position to another, all amid a pandemonium of shrieking and howling as men and horses and cattle succumbed to "the constant galling fire." Running about in a crouch from man to man, position to position, Washington had trouble keeping his balance on the already bloody ground. The French fire continued for hours with little or no interruption, and it was only the inaccuracy of the musketry that saved Fort Necessity from swift annihilation.

Late that afternoon the barrage was largely replaced by what Washington called "the most tremendous rain that can be conceived." The water poured into the meadow, driving the militiamen out of their trenches, drenching their powder and firelocks. About the only thing keeping the men going now was the rum being unofficially distributed from broken kegs. They were all, among other things, very hungry, but there was nothing more to eat, since Washington had been having the same kind of trouble with suppliers that he was destined to have a quarter of a century later.

At about dusk the French ceased firing, and across the meadow came a call, "Voulez-vous parler?" In response Washington sent out an interpreter under a white flag and then took the opportunity to walk about and assess his predicament. A third of his company were dead or wounded, arms and ammunition were in a precarious state, all the horses had been killed, and there was no food. Since he could presume that the French knew his situation was hopeless, he was pleasantly astonished when the interpreter came back to report that the French were offering extremely generous terms. If the defenders simply surrendered the fort, they could return home unmolested.

The commander of the French, the interpreter casually added, was the brother of the French captain, the "ambassador" who had been killed in Washington's earlier engagement. This seemed reason enough for the additional condition that the prisoners taken in that engagement must now be returned to the French. Perhaps it was this condition that lulled Washington from his habitual suspicion of anything French. Without it, he and his small staff might not have been hoodwinked.

For the captain's brother, a cunning fellow, had attached a preamble to the document of surrender. This French expedition, it explained, had been undertaken not to disturb the official peace existing between France and England but simply to requite the assassination of an official French messenger. Further along in the document this reference to an "assassination" was repeated. Thus Washington, in signing the document, was accepting the official view of the affair, not only because of the significant word but also because the document permitted the defenders' departure on the grounds that France and England were at peace, thereby implying that the French captain and his nine compatriots had been killed unlawfully. During the 160-mile trip back to Alexandria, McKay wrote later, Washington spoke not a single word.

When the document reached Paris, the French government eagerly and copiously distributed copies, and the ensuing uproar could easily be heard across the Atlantic. Paris resounded with attacks on London's perfidy, London with attacks on Washington's stupidity. His protests that his interpreter had translated "*l'assassinat*" as "death or loss" were noisily ignored as an ignoble effort to shift the blame. He was charged also with the loss of Indian support, considered vital to effective operation in the wilderness. And he thoroughly confirmed the British military establishment in its opinion of colonial officers as brave but foolhardy, well-intentioned but incompetent.

Over the next few months, while the French busily consolidated their gains in the Ohio valley and Washington tried desperately to defend his tattered reputation, Governor Dinwiddie arranged for the dissolution of the Virginia Regiment into its component companies, each to be commanded by a captain. Washington's

rank as regimental commander was thus neatly eliminated. Offered one of the captaincies, he indignantly and bitterly declined
the offer as humiliating, and resigned altogether. Disconsolate,
feeling thoroughly dishonored, he retired to his recently acquired
Mount Vernon to take up the life agricultural.

But in February 1755 a British major general named Edward
Braddock arrived in Virginia with a commission to capture Fort
Duquesne. He had been given two full regiments of regulars, to be
supported by such colonial forces as he could enlist in the cause.
Since he was about as familiar with the Ohio valley wilderness as
with the dark side of the moon, he needed, as an aide, someone
intimately acquainted with the territory. His staff made inquiries
and reported back to him: The outstanding candidate for the job
was a Virginia farmer, a former soldier named George Washington.

# Napoleon Bonaparte and the Fall of Robespierre

In Paris in the fall of 1793 Maximilien de Robespierre was riding high. As the leader of the radical Jacobin party, he had engineered the defeat of the more moderate Girondists, and his Jacobins had taken over the French government, such as it was. They had set up their infamous Committee of Public Safety and had begun their Reign of Terror, sending thousands of their dissident fellow countrymen to the guillotine and generally ruling the turbulent nation in a grip of paralyzing fear. It was at about this time that Maximilien's brother offered him a piece of advice: "If you should ever need an iron man for street fighting—a young man, a new man—then that man must be this Bonaparte."

"This Bonaparte," Major Napoleon Bonaparte, soon thereafter acquitted himself splendidly not merely in street fighting but in full-scale battle, defeating the English at Toulon in December. On his return to Paris he was promoted to brigadier general, given command of a military department, and commissioned to fortify the southeastern coast of France from Toulon to Nice. To supervise this operation, he moved to that area, with his main headquarters in Nice, from which he could visit Genoa. He was in Genoa on July 28, 1794, on a secret though legitimate mission.

Meanwhile things had not been going so well for his patron Robespierre. The Jacobins, in their frantic eagerness to eliminate political immorality, had stepped up the Terror during June and July. On July 26, in an eloquent but ambiguous speech before the National Convention, Robespierre seemed to urge moderation but at the same time threatened severe reprisals against his adversaries. This threat evidently was the last straw. It galvanized an already formed conspiracy of his political enemies, who on the following day joined firmly in a demand that the Convention order his arrest, which it did. He left Paris rather precipitously but was quickly captured. During the melee that accompanied his arrest, his jaw was shattered by a ball fired from a pistol. He was summarily sentenced to death and on July 28, his head covered with bandages, he lost it permanently to the guillotine.

The atmosphere in France at this time can hardly be described as one of live and let live. Robespierre's downfall boded ill for his supporters and for those thought to have been his supporters. This was even truer in the provinces than in Paris, since old enemies in the provinces were more isolated and could be picked off more easily. And so it was that Napoleon, on his return to Nice from Genoa, was placed under house arrest on a charge of conspiring with Robespierre and an assortment of plotters in Genoa to subvert the armed forces defending southern France. Relieved of all command, he could only watch as his quarters were searched and his official papers seized. A few close friends, visiting him later, urged him to take advantage of a plan they had devised for his escape, but he refused, relying on the complete lack of evidence against him and fearing that flight would be interpreted as a confession of guilt.

His confidence was vindicated when his chief accuser in the Convention, a fellow Corsican who had brought the charges to protect his own neck from excessive barbering, discovered that his neck was safe after all. He dropped all charges, swearing to the young general's innocence and patriotism. Within a week after his arrest, Napoleon was free.

But not restored to favor. Hearing that an expedition was being readied to confront the English in Corsica, the unemployed general rushed to Paris to ask for the command. He was rebuffed, ignored, snubbed. Two weeks later the miserable failure of this Corsican adventure reduced him to impotent despair. If they would not give him a command for which he was so obviously qualified and needed, what hope could he have for anything in the future? He wrote pleading letters to friends still in power. But they were now former friends, if indeed they would admit to having ever known him, and the letters bore no fruit.

Nor was the newly created establishment quite through with him yet. They offered him a command in the province of Vendée, on the west coast, far from the hub of political activity and any political support he might attract. Risking a charge of insubordination, he declined. They classified him as surplus in his beloved artillery, transferring him to the despised infantry. But, though unemployed and destitute, he stayed stubbornly in Paris.

The cost of living had risen several thousand percent since the early days of the Revolution five years before. His military pay had shrunk to a pittance. For as long as he could, he doled out most of it to support his mother and sisters and to pay a younger brother's school tuition. He cut down to one meal a day. He sold his carriage and took up lodgings in a Left Bank fleabag. In these disreputable surroundings his shabby uniform was all he had to wear—without the customary complement of gloves, which he could not afford.

Occasionally a friend would take him to see a play, although he regularly left early to avoid a happy ending, with which he was emotionally incompatible. When trapped by the requirements of etiquette into watching a comedy, he would sit in dour passivity amid the gales of laughter about him. It was not, at least entirely, an act. There are accounts of his trying to smile now and then but managing to produce only a kind of wry grimace. Such books as he read tended to reflect, and supplement, his melancholy. His disgrace, such as it was, was depressing. His idleness, with its feeling of uselessness, was devastating.

Time passed laboriously, hour by grudging hour. Without a proper home, without much food or decent clothing, without any identifiable prospects to offer him hope, he stood on the brink of a decline that threatened to plunge him irrevocably into an oblivion that, for him, would be a fate far worse than death. "Life," he wrote one day from the depths of his depression, "is an inconsequential dream, ever fading from our grasp." And again, in a letter to his brother Joseph, "If this keeps up, I shall end it by not stepping aside when a carriage speeds by." Not even his brief, though intense, romance with Désirée Clary seemed to cheer him up.

With the summer of 1795 there came a minor change in the government, a new war minister who wanted something done about the Italian front. After a search of the files revealed that this was Napoleon's area of expertise, he was called to the War Office. After a brilliant display of his detailed understanding of the situation, he was congratulated and asked for a written outline of his plans, which he submitted almost before the request could be completed. The plans are impressive, came the reaction, but impractical. They were shelved. But Napoleon was rewarded with a post in Operations.

Yet his tenure proved fleeting. The War Office harbored political enemies who felt threatened by the brash ambition of this all too able young officer. Eager to get him out of Paris, they arranged for him once again to be ordered to the provinces. And once again he insubordinately declined the honor. So, like his plans for the Italian campaign, he was shelved.

But not for long. Early in October Paris began to seethe with dissatisfaction over the National Convention's conduct of the government. Rioting broke out, and some 30,000 national guardsman lay siege to the Convention, which was protected by only about 5,000 troops, commanded by Vicomte Paul Barras, who had seen Napoleon in action at Toulon. Within hours Napoleon became Barras's assistant, assigned to defend the Convention against all comers.

Napoleon's instincts as an artilleryman were aroused by the overwhelming odds. If he was to defend the Convention, he must have some cannon. Preoccupied as he was with setting up makeshift fortifications, he was obliged to send a young cavalry officer named Murat to an arsenal six miles away, where he would find forty cannon and a store of ammunition. During that night of October 4 Murat and his troop of horsemen, barely getting to the arsenal and filching the vital armaments before the arrival of a formidable rebel force, delivered the guns at dawn, in time for Napoleon to place them strategically in his defenses—especially two eight-pounders that he pointed down a street from which he expected the main attack.

That afternoon a lavishly armed mob surged menacingly down the street toward the Convention. Napoleon waited for them quietly behind his deadly artillery. Suddenly the cannon barked out their famous "whiff of grapeshot," then again, and again, and within minutes the streets had been cleared of rebels, except for the dead and wounded. The national guardsmen, stunned and disorganized, lay down their arms. The rebellion was over within an hour of the first attack.

Napoleon was the hero of that hour. In a sense it was an hour destined to last, without significant interruption, for nearly twenty years.

# Simón Bolívar and Puerto Cabello

Simón Bolívar suffered many setbacks and some serious defeats before earning the title of Liberator and the Anglos' admiring description, "the George Washington of South America." But his greatest personal and professional failure, at least from his viewpoint at the time, was the loss of the fort at Puerto Cabello early in his career, in the summer of 1812.

A year earlier Venezuela's first representative congress had formally declared the country's independence from Spain after revolutionary forces under the command of Francisco de Miranda had taken over from the Spanish. But by early 1812 the "taking over" was proving inconclusive. By then the sixty-two-year-old Miranda had become dictator, apparently more interested in enjoying his perks than in preserving the First Republic of Venezuela. His immediate subordinates—including Bolívar, who was approaching thirty—found themselves growing ever more anxious over Generalissimo Miranda's tepid responses to the threat of Spanish royalist forces. A Spanish expeditionary force from the royal coastal town of Coro, commanded by Domingo Monteverde, was already nearing Barquisimeto, a revolutionary town less than a hundred miles west of the rebel's new capital, Valencia. Although it

46

was a small force of some 500 men, Monteverde had a reputation as a bold and aggressive commander. Furthermore, he would probably whip through the countryside like a knife through water, since the peasants were worn out and disillusioned by economic convulsions—loss of markets due to the Spanish blockade, raging inflation, poverty deteriorating into destitution.

But the economic convulsions were mild compared to the seismic convulsions that rocked the land on March 26. It was one of the most destructive earthquakes ever to batter that quake-ridden region. Tens of thousands were killed, hundreds of thousands injured, scores of towns destroyed. In the bleak aftermath, amid the rubble and the groans of pain and moans of bereavement, royalist politicians and clerics tonguelashed the survivors for supporting or tolerating the atheistic revolution that had provoked almighty God into this paroxysm of punishment. By the time that Monteverde entered the pile of rubble that had been Barquisimeto, any thoughts of resistance had faded into a passive resignation. In Valencia, or what remained of it, popular indignation against the revolution grew so hot that the troops assigned to defend the town were forced to leave before Monteverde arrived.

This desertion of Valencia was especially galling to Bolívar, who had hoped, even expected, to be entrusted with its defense. When Miranda ordered him instead to defend Puerto Cabello, situated on the coast a few miles north of Valencia, he interpreted the order as a sign of distrust in his military competence. Actually, Miranda may have considered the town more important than Valencia, since the port could provide a channel for any supplies that he might hope to receive from overseas. Further, just outside the town was an important fort holding a large store of supplies and arms as well as many important royalist prisoners. And Monteverde's troops were alarmingly close to it.

This was an alternative interpretation of Miranda's order, at any rate, although the generalissimo may have been too concerned with his personal future to give much thought to strategy. Instead of counterattacking against Monteverde's much smaller force, he slowly retreated eastward toward Caracas, meanwhile subjecting his troops to such untimely training disciplines as close-order drill. The desertions prompted by this fiddling were aggravated by a huge loss of supplies and ammunition when Monteverde out-flanked him to the north and south and forced him to fall back to Victoria, the last major town on the way to Caracas. Here he managed to bring the weary troops of Monteverde to a halt. And here he resumed his fiddling while some of his younger officers began casting about for a way to replace him.

Meanwhile Bolívar fumed restlessly in Puerto Cabello while reports flowed into his office with news of Miranda's lethargic withdrawal. At one point he sent the generalissimo a message recommending that he be allowed to lead a contingent of troops to a region behind Monteverde, who was overextended and might be persuaded to concentrate on protecting his rear. But Miranda was not interested. Nor did he seem much interested now in the defense of Puerto Cabello, although Bolívar had protested against keeping valuable prisoners in a place so likely to be attacked, especially since their presence made the fort that much more important as a prize of war. Some of the defensive positions around the fort had already fallen, and Bolívar was growing ever more concerned.

What he did not need at this point was a rebellion, or counterrebellion, but that is what he got. The prisoners had inveigled an officer of the guard and some of his men to help them take over the fort. At noon on June 30 Bolívar, then at his headquarters in the town, was told that the royal flag had been hoisted over the fort. With only a few men at his disposal, there was nothing he could do. Soon the fort began bombarding the town. Bolívar sent the fort's occupiers a rather presumptuous message offering them amnesty if they would surrender, but they knew as well as he that he was overwhelmingly outmanned and outgunned. The shelling continued through the night, and at 3:00 A.M. Bolívar sent Miranda a message announcing that he would hold out as long as possible but would inevitably have to surrender the town unless Miranda sent him some help. He received no response.

During the next day the fort poured shells into the town at such a rate that the people began hastily leaving it, along with many of Bolívar's less dedicated soldiers. On July 6, now outnumbered ten to one, he also left the city along with the surviving defenders and sailed a hundred miles east to La Guaira and the adjacent Caracas. In his camp near Victoria Miranda, on receiving news of the defeat, told his staff that Venezuela had been "wounded to the heart." Then, theatrics over, he relapsed into his infuriating apathy—in which, at least, he did not indulge in recriminations over Bolívar's retreat.

He did not have to. Bolívar spent the next several days in self-recrimination. He was acutely aware of making a painfully careless mistake in allowing the royalist prisoners to be kept in the fort together with the great bulk of his supplies and ammunition. The combination had proved lethal after a bit of treason had supplied the catalyst, and his failure to anticipate the catalyst simply compounded the blame that he heaped upon himself. On July 12 he sent a note to Miranda accepting full responsibility for the loss of the port and asking to be demoted to the equivalent of shavetail. No response.

That same day Miranda informed his war council that he had sued for peace. During the negotiations occupying the next two weeks he found time to arrange for his escape on a ship out of La Guaira, together with such money and other valuables as he could take along. Although he seemed obsessed with escape, however, even in this his lethargy undid him. When he arrived at the port on July 30, after surrendering all Venezuela to Monteverde, he decided, against the ship's captain's advice, to spend a last night in the town. This was a fateful decision, since his official family, especially Bolívar, increasingly suspected that he was engaged in a leisurely but well prepared getaway attempt, which had to be thwarted. After dinner with him that evening, in a meeting with the military commander of La Guaira and other functionaries, they determined to arrest him. The next morning they did so, imprisoning him in a nearby fort. When Monteverde occupied Caracas and La Guaira, the commander turned the fort over to him with Miranda still in it. Miranda died in a prison in Cadiz two years later.

Monteverde violated all the terms of the general agreement of surrender, throwing into prison every important revolutionary he could flush out. Bolívar hid in the house of a friend until another friend, Francisco Iturbe, agreed to use his influence with the victorious Monteverde to obtain an exit visa permitting Bolívar to leave Venezuela. Monteverde, who had been more impressed with Bolívar's revolutionary ardor at Puerto Cabello than had Miranda, at first refused. Iturbe offered himself as guarantor (an act that served him well with the Liberator years later). Monteverde softened, and Iturbe suggested bringing Bolívar to him for an interview. At this meeting Monteverde agreed to issue the visa as a reward for Bolívar's leading role in the arrest of Miranda. Bolívar, stiffening, answered that he had been involved in that arrest because of Miranda's treason against his country, not against the king. Monteverde canceled the visa. Irturbe persisted. Monteverde again relented, reluctantly and surprisingly. Bolívar left Venezuela without further imprudence, or impudence.

At the port, however, because of some flaw in the ship's papers, all his personal property, everything but what he was wearing, was confiscated. He sailed nevertheless, arriving in Cartegena (in Nueva Granada to the west, still held by the rebels) destitute and known chiefly for his surrender of Puerto Cabello, and for his contribution thereby to Spain's reconquest of Venezuela. It was not his most brightly shining hour.

But he turned out to be a man tempered by adversity, the kind of leader that the revolution in South America desperately needed. His zeal now for the liberation not only of Venezuela but of all South America was white hot, and the atrocities committed by Spanish royalists on helpless colonists made that zeal especially contagious. With the support of the western rebels he led an army into Venezuela, forced his way to Caracas, and, in August 1813, liberated his native land. For the next eleven years he smote the Spanish on one battlefield after another, suffering defeats—including a disastrous one from which he had to flee to Haiti—but also, increasingly, gaining some victories.

His final victory, in 1824, brought the end of Spanish power in South America. And in those later years the story was that Monteverde, whenever he heard Bolívar's name, and that was quite often, grew pale.

# Gioacchino Rossini and *The Barber of Seville*

T hrough a convergence of misunderstandings, misfortunes, and mishaps, the first performance of Gioacchino Rossini's *Barber of Seville* was an unalloyed disaster.

That first performance took place on the evening of February 20, 1816. Two months earlier Rossini had accepted a contract to write a new opera for the Teatro di Argentina in Rome. The theater was owned by a Roman aristocrat, Duca Francesco Sforza-Cesarini, who had spent much of the family fortune on his theater, his love for opera, and his satisfying role as impresario. He had indeed spent so much of it that he could not give Rossini as much support as either man would have liked, especially in the way of competent performers and stagehands and enough rehearsal time.

Another problem was with the libretto. The first one given serious consideration was finally rejected as too trite, and the second was accepted largely because time was slipping by alarmingly. Yet in a sense the second threatened to be as trite as the first, since it was based on a widely known French play, by Beaumarchais, *The Barber of Seville,* and used many of the characters from Mozart's *Marriage of Figaro.* Furthermore, it invited direct comparison with another Italian opera, then very popular, composed by one Giovanni Paisiello and also entitled *The Barber of Seville.*

Rossini got around the Paisiello problem by writing that composer a note to the effect that he had no wish to compete with anyone so conspicuously his superior and that, as a token of his deference, he intended to change the title of his opera to *Almaviva,* after one of the leading characters. More accurately, Rossini got around Paisiello but not the problem. Paisiello replied to him graciously enough, assuring him that the matter was inconsequential (as inconsequential as he privately expected Rossini's opera to be). But the precursor *Barber* had many devoted fans in Rome who were to prove less amiable, or indifferent.

The libretto for *Almaviva* did not reach Rossini until mid-January. He began work on the music on the eighteenth and, with the help of a few extracts from some of his earlier operas, delivered the completed manuscript to the theater only three weeks later, on February 6, for the first rehearsal, scheduled for February 7. Then came a stroke of bad luck, the death of Sforza-Cesarini during the night of February 6–7. The duke's financial condition proved worse than expected, and now it would be up to the opera to help support his widow and children.

In that respect they could not have been greatly encouraged by the opening night. The performance was ruled by Murphy's Law, to the raucous delight of a large group of pro-Paisiello (and anti-Rossini) fanatics who seemed to make up half or more of the audience. Even before it started, when Rossini appeared at the cembalo, or harpsichord, wearing a light grayish brown outfit sporting gold buttons, he was greeted with hoots and hollers and piercing whistles (the Italian equivalent of boos), as though no one so accoutred could be remotely capable of making any music worth listening to. Nevertheless, the curtain went up on schedule.

The first scene evidently was played through without any serious problem other than a kind of seething counterpoint from the audience, but the second introduced disaster. Don Basilio, on his entrance, tripped on a trapdoor and sprawled flat on his face. After a moment of stunned inertia, he scrambled to his feet. The audience could see that his face was painfully scratched, and his nose, gushing blood, was nearly broken. The unsympathetic audience, or at least the unsympathetic portion of the audience, an observer later reported, "like its ancestors in the Colosseum, viewed that flow of blood with joy." There was an "abominable hubbub" of laughter and applause, laced with demands that the poor singer "do it again."

Another part of the audience, assuming that the belly flop was a deliberate piece of stage business, a banana peel interpretation of the role, loudly defended the performer against his clamorous critics. Although this protest added to the general uproar, it suffered the fate of most minority reports. Meanwhile the company continued with the opera, rather doggedly. And the partisans continued with their clamor.

Don Basilio's famous aria on the effects of gossip, which followed soon after his flying entrance, was punctuated with pauses during which he tried to staunch the flow of blood from his nose with a fast-reddening handkerchief. His efforts to do so were greeted every time by derisive laughter, whistles, catcalls, and other such commentary from the musical guerrillas throughout the theater. The aria rose to its splendidly feverish climax, and at that moment a cat, perhaps released by a partisan, appeared on stage and joined the performance in a state of some confusion. Figaro managed to shoo it offstage and into the right wing, but it soon reappeared from the left wing and took a flying leap at Dr. Bartolo, who despite his paunch caught it as skillfully as though catching flying cats were his offstage profession. He was unable to hold it, however, and soon it was in pursuit of Berta the housemaid, who showed equal skill in ducking and weaving in her frightened efforts to avoid being scratched. By this time the audience, friends and foes alike, were in the grip of paroxysms of helpless laughter, and the cathartic pandemonium continued until the appearance on stage of the police, which occurs near the end of the first act. Then, finally, the captain of the patrol frightened away the feline interloper with his sword.

Through all this and the rest of his uncontrollably comic opera Rossini sat at his cembalo almost impassively, playing on cue but otherwise feigning indifference to the deafening melee and to the torrents of personal insults. At the end of the first act, however, he rose and loudly, defiantly applauded the long-suffering but stalwart performers. After the final curtain he crept home alone and as inconspicuously as possible. There he altered the score in the hope of making the opera less vulnerable. The next night, anxious to avoid further humiliation, he stayed home on a pretext of illness.

But the second performance was a success, respectable if not resounding. The partisans evidently had shot their bolt on opening night, and this evening's audience was well behaved and very appreciative. Yet the opera's reception was not favorable enough for a long engagement: it ran for seven nights in Rome, till the end of the season, and was not produced there again for five years. Meanwhile it began touring Italy and the rest of Europe under its restored title, *The Barber of Seville.*

The critics generally were lukewarm. In England they branded the music as frivolous, predicting that the opera soon would be lost in the mists of oblivion. A German critic thought it inferior to Paisiello's work and, of all things, found the music ponderous. In France some also compared Rossini's opera unfavorably with Paisiello's, while others condemned it as deficient in singable tunes. Many of Rossini's fellow composers, however—including Beethoven, Berlioz, Brahms, and Wagner—praised it highly. Wagner, although he disliked much of Rossini's music, described this *Barber* as the most beautiful comic opera ever written. And opera lovers ever since generally seem to agree with him.

# Samuel F. B. Morse and the Telegraph

O n a fateful evening in March 1843, as he awaited a decision that could change his life, Samuel F. B. Morse might well have reflected that he was no stranger to defeat, failure, or frustration.

Early in life he had wanted to be an artist. His father tried to stifle this ambition throughout his son's late teens but, succumbing to the boy's persistence, allowed him in 1811, at the age of twenty, to go to London to study. There the young man met with another kind of resistance, from the Royal Academy of Art, whose entrance examiners found his work inadequate for admission. Daunted but not defeated, Morse settled down to a life of hard work and severe frugality. After two years of this he sounded very much the destitute artist. "I have had no new clothes for nearly a year," he wrote. "My best are threadbare, my shoes are out at the toes, my stockings all want to see my mother."

But his luck turned. He did gain admission to the Academy, and some of his work began to bring him favorable notice. He entered a clay figure of Hercules in a competition, and it won a gold medal. At least two of his paintings were included in very reputable exhibitions. In 1815 he decided that he was ready to embark on a career back in America. And indeed he may have been ready, but America was not.

His paintings were too much in the European fashion of the time, too ardently devoted to romantic subjects taken from classical mythology (*The Dying Hercules, The Judgment of Jupiter*) for any warm acceptance in hard-headed America. They met with a polite indifference, which demoralized Morse so thoroughly that his father became alarmed, writing a friend that his son's ambition and spirits were in danger of falling into an "ultimate sink." Although the young painter tended to look down his nose at portrait painting, he now found himself doing portraits of his brothers and grandparents, and even of himself. And, although not so grand as pictures of Hercules and Jupiter, these paintings turned out very well indeed.

And so he spent the next ten years wandering about New England, New York, and then South Carolina, painting portraits all along the way and getting paid for them. His portraits began to earn him a reputation because they were more realistic than was currently fashionable. They had a spittin' image quality that appealed to American tastes, although the Romanticism that he had absorbed in Europe kept them from giving offense in the warts-'n'-all tradition. By 1818 his reputation was secure enough to earn him a left-handed compliment that doubtless softened the impact of a somewhat peripheral failure.

Some time before this he and his brother Sidney had developed a water pump, which, because of its power, they facetiously dubbed "Morse's Patent Metallic Double-Headed Ocean-Drinker and Deluge-Spouter Valve Pump Box." With backing from a speculator they had built and sold many small versions as "small engines for gardens and streets," and one full-sized version for use in a fire engine. The Massachusetts town of Concord bought the large version, which the local paper described as less expensive and more efficient than another candidate for purchase: "It requires much less manual labor, and throws the water to as great a distance and in as large quantities." In its first official test, however, it failed to produce so much as a squirt, and Morse's fiancée, then living in Concord, had to write to him in Charlestown as gently as possible about the spectators' sardonic reactions, including the ambiguous compliment, "Mr. Morse had better stick to his brush, he will do well enough then."

And indeed he did do well enough, although he evidently found it rather hard to stick to his brush because of his nagging feeling that portrait painting could never be anything better than merely a way to earn a living. But in 1825, after his brief marriage had ended with the death of his young wife, he returned to New York, where he was deluged with commissions. Perhaps because many of these portraits were of friends, including the Marquis de Lafayette, Governor DeWitt Clinton, and William Cullen Bryant, they have survived as some of the finest work ever done by an American artist.

Yet there were not many people with enough affluence and motivation to want their portraits done. The flood of private commissions slowly ebbed, and by 1837 Morse was pinning his hopes on a government commission to decorate the Capitol rotunda with historical paintings. In that year Congress appointed a committee to select four artists to do the job, and Morse, who was then president of the National Academy of Design, expected to be one of them. To his despair, when the committee named seven artists who were to submit preliminary sketches, he was not among them. Nor was he among the four finally chosen. John Quincy Adams, a member of the committee, had argued that the competition should be open to foreign artists because they were superior to American artists, and an acidly critical response had been published as a letter in the *Evening Post*. Adams thought Morse had written the letter (which had actually been written by Morse's friend, James Fenimore Cooper). When one of the four artists selected offered his resignation in favor of Morse, Adams persuaded him to withdraw the offer. Morse took his humiliation hard and blamed it, understandably, on Adams. "He killed me as a painter," he wrote, "and he intended to do it."

Yet later he found in this failure the seeds of success, since it turned him toward another pursuit. Five years earlier, aboard ship on his return from a brief visit to Europe, he and several acquaintances joined in a conversation that touched on the recently discovered phenomenon of electromagnetism. He learned that, for all practical purposes (this was a century and a half ago, before electronic computers), electricity would pass through a wire instantaneously. The length of the wire would make no difference, and this meant, he had suddenly realized, that messages might be transmitted over long distances and received at virtually the same instant. Although others had had this idea before him, he thought it was original with him, and he found it very exciting. He spent the rest of the trip home feverishly pursuing it in his thoughts, in his notebook, and in conversations with his fellow passengers. By the time the ship pulled into New York harbor, the phrase "electric telegraph" had become embedded in his vocabulary. His head and his notebooks were filled with designs and schemes. He was elated, thoroughly exhilarated.

His high spirits plummeted, however, as he encountered the practical difficulties involved in developing a demonstration model. He needed miles of insulated wire, for example; since such wire was not available on reels, he had to buy uninsulated wire in short lengths, weld these lengths end to end, and painstakingly wrap them in cotton thread. Over the next five years, despite the distractions of intermittent painting, amateur politics, and genteel poverty, he managed to produce a model for a demonstration in 1837. The potential investors in the audience found the device clever in concept but rather fragile and insubstantial in construction. They considered the demonstration entertaining but they would not invest a dime in any effort to market the invention. Morse was crushed. In both of his areas of major interest, a single year had seen his hopes culminate in utter failure. He decided to concentrate on his telegraph.

Over the next five years, despite some help from his brothers

Richard and Sidney, and despite a more impressive demonstration model built by his friend Alfred Vail, Morse could find no financial backing. In 1838 he demonstrated the Vail model at a congressional hearing in Washington, but to no avail. He traveled to England and France in search of investors, but without any success. In 1842 he laboriously strung together two miles of wire, which he had, also laboriously, waterproofed with tar, pitch, and rubber. On an October morning he rowed across New York harbor, from the Battery to Governors Island, playing out the wire to lie along the bottom. That evening he sent a message across the harbor in a successful trial, and the next morning the *New York Herald* announced that a demonstration would be held at noon. But during the morning a ship caught its anchor in the wire, and the crew, after raising the wire, cut it as a piece of interfering debris. The expectant crowd that had gathered at the Battery greeted Morse's embarrassed announcement with catcalls.

Shortly thereafter Morse somehow borrowed enough money to go to Washington, where New York's Representative Charles Ferris had introduced a bill to appropriate $30,000 to test the electric telegraph. This time the Committee on Commerce reported the bill to the House with a favorable recommendation, but its prospects on the floor, where a budget-cutting drive was in progress, were by no means favorable. As Morse wandered through the Capitol day after day, waiting, he could view the panoply of historical paintings to which he had hoped to contribute his talents. As December 1842 faded into January 1843 Morse visited the House gallery more often and more anxiously. The session was scheduled to end on March 3. It was not until February 21 that his bill reached the floor. After two agonizing days of debates, delays, and amendments, the bill was passed by a narrow margin and sent to the Senate. Perhaps significantly, its support had come entirely from states north of the Mason-Dixon line.

Since the Senate already had more on its plate than it could conveniently handle, Morse had to go through the waiting process all over again. February faded into March. On the morning of March 3 Morse arrived at the Senate for an anxious day. He waited through the day and into the evening. A few senators came by to prepare him for the bad news: The bill might never reach the floor, and, if it did, it might well be defeated. Finally Morse could take no more. He returned to his small hotel room dreading the thought of again returning to New York to report failure and to face another year of hopeless struggle. Checking at the hotel desk, he discovered that he had just enough money to pay the bill and buy a ticket to New York, with thirty-seven cents left over. But he did manage to sleep that night. The tension may have exhausted him.

The next morning he had a visitor, the daughter of the Commissioner of Patents. She had shown a friendly interest in the fate of his bill through its successive congressional crises, and now she told him that she had come to congratulate him. When she saw that he really did not understand—she evidently had not expected to be the first to bring him the news—she explained that at the last moment his bill had passed the Senate and been signed by the president.

Not long afterward Morse borrowed fifty dollars and bought some new clothes. His credit had greatly improved.

# Mary Godwin and *Frankenstein*

M ary Godwin's early life was rather spooky. Her father, the doctrinaire philosopher William Godwin, had left the ministry to devote himself to promulgating the ideas of the Enlightenment, especially the perfectibility of mankind, and to cultivating a degree of poverty that made life quite gloomy for his family. Her stepmother seems to have been modeled on Cinderella's (at least as seen through the fractious Mary's eyes). The rest of the family included a stepsister given to alternating periods of flightiness and hysteria, and a half-sister whose oppressive melancholy eventually led to suicide. Amid all this perhaps the greatest influence on her was her own mother (Mary Wollstonecraft), who had died in bringing her into the world, thereby cutting short a career as a writer and influential feminist. Mary evidently could never quite shake the feeling that she had murdered her mother, however inadvertently. She spent a great deal of time at the grave in a nearby cemetery, reading and meditating and, by her own account, talking with her mother.

Yet her home offered plenty of intellectual stimulation for a person of her natural intelligence. She was surrounded by books and learned a love of reading, especially about the occult. In 1805, when she was eight, her father was prodded by her stepmother into forming a company publishing books especially for young people. Although never a financial success, it did publish books of good quality—Charles and Mary Lamb's *Tales from Shakespeare* and the first English edition of *The Swiss Family Robinson*—and it graced the Godwins' home with literati (the Lambs, William Hazlitt, Robert Southey, Samuel Coleridge, William Wordsworth) with whom the precocious Mary quickly learned to hold her own in easy conversation.

She met Percy Bysshe Shelley at the age of sixteen. He was twenty-one, trapped in a miserable marriage. A month before her seventeenth birthday they ran off together, taking along Claire, the flighty stepsister, who was just the kind of ineffectual chaperone that they preferred. (They were married late in 1816, after Shelley's first wife had committed suicide.) In May 1816 they left England for Europe, settling eventually in a rented house facing Lake Geneva. Claire, who like scores of other women had fallen as deeply in love with the spectacular Lord Byron as her shallow nature allowed, and who had become his mistress, invited herself along when she learned that Byron also was leaving England for Europe. Indeed, she went so far as to invite him to join them in Geneva.

He did so in May, arriving with a friend, a young physician named John Polidori, and immediately rented the house next door. Although the Shelleys, incredibly, disapproved of Claire's intimacy with Byron, there was nothing they could do about it, and they soon became so fond of Byron, and he of them, that his relationship with Claire faded into irrelevancy. The five neighbors, thoroughly compatible, quickly became constant, and incorrigibly boon, companions. They were colorful celebrities now, scandalously so, and tourists in the area that summer began carrying stories back to England of the indiscriminate orgies and various other titillating carryings-on in the two houses, much to the Shelleys' indignation and Byron's weary indifference.

Actually, there were some carryings-on, but of a character much different from the steamy activities bubbling away in the tourists' imaginations. The two couples and the doctor shared a fascination with the occult, intensified by the then fashionable preoccupation with gothic romances. Their evenings therefore were filled with seances and later, as their imaginations began churning, with the telling of ghost stories and other horror tales. As the stories became more gruesome, the participants became more excited. Claire reacted hysterically with increasing frequency, and one evening Shelley suddenly leaped up and rushed through the house, filling it with terrified screams, until the others finally were able to hold him while the doctor bound and gagged him, after which it took Mary an hour to calm him down enough to release him.

This so alarmed the storytellers that they decided to take another, gentler approach to reciprocal terrorizing. Each of them, they agreed, would write a story dealing with the supernatural. Mary, however, was the only one to take the agreement seriously. Claire had neither the talent nor the interest needed for such a sustained effort, and the two poets were otherwise creatively engaged. (Byron's "Prisoner of Chillon" and Shelley's "Hymn to Intellectual Beauty" were products of this period.) Polidori did come up with a short tale entitled *The Vampyre*, but a suspicion existed, and lingers, that it may have been virtually dictated by Byron. As for Mary, her creative juices seemed at the ready, but she could not channel them into anything specific. All she needed was a plot and some appropriate characters, but they remained beyond reach somewhere in her unconscious. When Shelley asked her each morning whether she had started her story, she could only look at him blankly and shake her head in despair.

An end to her frustration came one evening during a conversation on the nature and origin of life. Byron and Shelley discussed phenomena such as the electrical animation of organic matter, and their animation seemed to animate Mary's dormant imagination. "Perhaps," she wrote later in describing her reaction, "a corpse could be re-animated; galvanism had given token of such things: perhaps the component parts of a creature might be manufactured, brought together, and endued with vital warmth."

Night waned upon this talk [she continued], and even the witching hour had gone by, before we retired. When I placed my head upon my pillow, I did not sleep, nor could I be said to think. My imagination, unbidden, possessed and guided me, gifting the successive images that arose in my mind with a vividness far beyond the usual bounds of reverie. I saw, with shut eyes but acute mental vision—I saw the pale student of unhallowed arts kneeling beside the thing he had put together. I saw the hideous phantasm of a man stretched out, and then, on the working of some powerful engine, show signs of life, and stir with an uneasy, half vital motion.... [The student] sleeps; but he is awakened; he opens his eyes; behold, the horrid thing stands at his bedside, opening his curtains, and looking on him with yellow, watery, but speculative eyes.

The next morning she told Shelley of her dream, or vision, and announced that she hoped to make a short story out of it. Shelley, delighted, encouraged her, adding that she probably had enough material, with some embellishment, for a full-length novel. She began writing with deep misgivings, but after she had written a few chapters and had the poets read them, Byron joined Shelley in his enthusiastic encouragement. She continued doggedly, retiring into her study to write every day from ten to two, to the idle Claire's chagrin. She finished the rough draft in the spring of 1817 and by the middle of May, with editorial help from her husband, she had laboriously written out a presentable copy. But was it publishable? Would anybody read it? To enhance its chances in both respects, in view of the prevailing bias against female authors, the three writers decided that it should be published anonymously and that Shelley and Byron should submit it to publishers as "the work of a friend." They all returned to England in August.

First to receive the manuscript was Byron's publisher, who turned it over to a reader, who recommended rejection. Too far out. Then Shelley sent it to his publisher, who bounced it back immediately. This cavalier treatment was discouraging enough for the Shelleys to consider submitting the manuscript to a publisher of cheap bestsellers, including novels with sensational, occult themes. They did so. The publisher expressed some interest, but so reluctantly that Shelley had to offer a special deal on royalties as bait. The publisher agreed to the deal in September, and *Frankenstein* was published in March 1818.

Generally the early reviews, when good, were not so good, but when they were bad they were horrid. One described the book as a "wild and hideous tale," and another condemned it as "a tissue of horrible and disgusting absurdity" and a "tale told by an idiot, full of sound and fury, signifying nothing," with the author leaving the reader "in doubt whether he is not as mad as his hero." (The "hero" is Victor Frankenstein, of course, not the monster.) This second reviewer confessed to some admiration for a few of the book's passages, but "when we have thus admitted that *Frankenstein* has pages which appall the mind and make the flesh creep, we have given it all the praise (if praise it can be called) which we dare to bestow." The book, he predicted, "will not even amuse its readers, unless their taste has been deplorably vitiated—it fatigues the feelings without interesting the understanding; it gratuitously harasses the heart, and only adds to the store, already too great, of painful sensations." Still another reviewer, although he discerned some "beauties" among "all the faults" of the book, concluded in the end that "we do not well see why it should have been written."

Mary's disappointment was alleviated, however, by some good news from her publisher. The book was beginning to sell far better than had been expected. And then the reviews began improving. A conservative journal considered the book "impious" but also ingenious, daring, and excellently written. Another described it as "an extraordinary tale, in which the author seems to disclose uncommon powers of poetic imagination." This review was especially gratifying to Mary, since it was written by Sir Walter Scott, who graced it further with the comment that he preferred the novel to any of his own.

Yet, despite the subsequent enormous popular, critical, and financial success of *Frankenstein*, one aspect of the reaction to it in these early days must have been galling to the daughter of Mary Wollstonecraft. Permeating all the reviews, including Scott's, and all the public comment was the unspoken assumption that a horror story so vigorously written, displaying such intelligence, could not have been written by a mere woman. Even after the 1831 edition came out under her name (Mary Shelley, for this was her preference), the assumption persisted for many years. But her fame outlived it.

# Walt Whitman and
# *Leaves of Grass*

In October 1854 an obscure journalist, printer's helper, carpenter, and poet, all rather loosely jumbled within one personality, addressed a "Memorial in Behalf of a Freer Municipal Government, and Against Sunday Restrictions" to the city council of Brooklyn. The council had recently passed some blue laws that prohibited the operation of public transportation on Sundays. These pious ordinances denied to most working people the opportunity to visit parks and other recreational areas on their only day off. It was appropriate that Walt Whitman should write a vigorous protest against the puritan establishment's insistence that ordinary American noses be kept to the plutocracy's grindstone twelve hours a day, six days a week, and to God's on the seventh day, to be kept holy by enforced self-denial. And it was significant of the environment, if not appropriate, that his memorial, although presented to the mayor by the council and published in a local newspaper, received no popular support. Believers in masochistic piety were not limited to the elite.

Whitman's defense, indeed his glorification, of the ordinary people with whom he so closely identified found expression the following year in the first edition of *Leaves of Grass*. The irony of

68

its reception is that such acclaim as it received came solely from the literary elite. Its reception by ordinary readers is reflected in a slight exaggeration voiced by Whitman in later years, to the effect that not a single copy was sold. At least it was true that not a single commercial publisher would have anything to do with the manuscript. But as a sometime printer Whitman had some friends in that trade, including James and Thomas Rome, whose shop printed mostly legal works but who were willing to print his poems, especially in view of his eager assistance with such chores as setting type and providing the necessary funds. (On the source of these funds the record is unclear.)

During July 1855 a small ad appeared each day in the *New York Tribune* announcing the availability of "Walt Whitman's Poems, 'Leaves of Grass,' 1 vol. small quarto, $2" to what Whitman hoped would be an eager public. It was a thin volume in green cover, ornately filigreed as was the custom; its hundred pages or so contained twelve poems printed in a free verse typography that must have looked mighty peculiar in the tightly ordered world of Victorian America. Of the thousand copies printed, perhaps a third were clothbound, a few more paperbound, and most not bound at all. Purchased copies were overwhelmingly outnumbered by complimentary copies. The sale has been described by one literary chronicler as the most resounding flop in the history of American literature.

One of the free copies went to Ralph Waldo Emerson, who was a bit of a hero to Whitman. The great man found it absorbing. After all, in the preface and in much of the poetry he found Whitman saying eloquently what he himself had been saying for years, as well as a great deal that he had not said but did agree with enthusiastically. In return for his complimentary copy he sent Whitman a much more complimentary letter acknowledging the work as "the most extraordinary piece of wit and wisdom that America has yet contributed," marking "the beginning of a great career." Whitman carried the letter around with him everywhere for several months, partly as balm for the wounds inflicted by some more public comments.

As an example of the latter, a rather pretentious weekly published in New York City, the *Criterion,* sniffed at the poems as "a mess of stupid filth," passing off the report of Emerson's admiration as just one more case in which "an ill-considered letter of introduction has oftentimes procured the admittance of a scurvy fellow into good society." Obviously this critic was no uninhibited admirer of the common folk eulogized by Whitman, nor could anyone capable of exuding such laborious prose be likely to enjoy the freely swinging style displayed so exuberantly in *Leaves*—nor would someone so precise be irresistibly attracted to the self-portrait that appears in the first of the poems:

> Walt Whitman, an American, one of the roughs,
>     a kosmos,
> Disorderly fleshly and sensual.... eating
>     drinking and breeding,
> No sentimentalist.... no stander above men
>     and women or apart from them.... no
>     more modest than immodest.

The book's reviews were not as disastrous as its sales. Charles Dana, in the *New York Tribune,* appreciated the poems' originality "in their external forms" and "the vigor and quaint beauty of isolated portions." But he did object to the "indecent" language, it being of a kind that Adam and Eve might have used, he speculated, before the need arose for fig leaves. Charles Eliot Norton in *Putnam's Magazine* shrugged off the poems as "a mixture of Yankee transcendentalism and New York rowdyism" which blended literary conceits in such confusion as to make "an otherwise striking passage altogether laughable." John Greenleaf Whittier, it was reported, had burned his complimentary copy.

These were among the discouragingly few reviews—so few that Whitman resorted to writing three anonymous, or pseudonymous, reviews himself ("An American bard at last!"), succumbing to a practice unblinkingly common among authors a century or more ago. He also got Dana to publish Emerson's letter in the *Tribune*, without notifying Emerson beforehand, in a bit of self-puffery that Emerson considered rude but not unforgivable. And in the second edition of *Leaves of Grass*, published in the fall of 1856, there was the Emerson letter again, conspicuously on display. So desperately did Whitman yearn for readers.

The second edition netted him very few, despite a torrent of elaborate praise from Fanny Fern, a prodigiously popular columnist of the time. Her adulation did nothing to sell his poetry because the poetry seemed to be of peripheral interest to her. In the spring of 1856 she wrote that she had not read Whitman the poet but had met Whitman the man—and, oh, those shoulders, that "muscular throat," and the voice, "rich, deep, and clear as a clarion note." The man doubtless appreciated this more than the poet, whose singing still remained largely unsung.

He was, however, a colorful character whose nonconformist poetry had become an enduring conversation piece at social gatherings of the literary elite. This doubtless kept his reputation alive and the copies of the *Leaves* (mostly complimentary) in circulation. It may also partly explain a letter he received in February 1860 from a new abolitionist publishing firm in Boston, the kind of letter that aspiring writers dream about: "Dear Sir, We want to be the publishers of Walt. Whitman's poems. . . . Are you writing other poems? Are they ready for press? Will you let us read them? Will you write us?"—and so on. Whitman did write them, and the third edition of *Leaves of Grass*, fat with many new poems, was published only a few months later. It did much better in sales than the first two editions, as would each of the many editions in the years to come—increasingly. Walt Whitman took some getting used to.

In 1916 a book by Henry B. Rankin told of a man more celebrated than Whitman who had shown an early appreciation of his work. This reader had found the poems in *Leaves of Grass* remarkable for "their virility, freshness, unconventional sentiments, and unique forms of expression, [promising] a new school of poetry"—although he added that he "had barely saved it from being purified by fire by the women." The reader was Abraham Lincoln.

# Abraham Lincoln and the Election of 1858

It was the summer of 1858, less than eight years before the Thirteenth Amendment would free all the slaves everywhere in the United States. The proslavery Democrats had a grip on the federal government that seemed unbreakable. In 1854 a Democratic leader in the Senate, Stephen A. Douglas of Illinois, had negotiated the passage of the Kansas-Nebraska Act, which in effect repealed the Missouri Compromise of 1820 and opened the new territories west of the Mississippi to the introduction of chattel slavery. Three years later, in March 1857, the predominantly Democratic Supreme Court had thrown its enormous weight behind the proslavery viewpoint with its Dred Scott decision, which declared that the Missouri Compromise had always been unconstitutional and that the federal government did not have the authority to forbid slavery in any territory. Neither, the decision implied, did the territorial legislatures, as creatures of the federal government, have any such authority.

It was also the summer of 1858 that saw Stephen Douglas campaigning in Illinois for reelection to his Senate seat against an obscure politician unknown outside the state, a member of the new Republican party named Abraham Lincoln. Not long before this, Douglas had won favor with many Republicans by taking a stand against a political fraud engineered by proslavery Democrats in Kansas. Although he held to the doctrine of "popular sovereignty" that left the slavery question to the popular vote in each new territory or state, the "popular" vote for a proslavery constitution in Kansas had been so obviously rigged that he courageously condemned it. As a result, eastern Republicans were pressing Illinois Republicans to support him in his campaign for reelection.

Like many other Illinois Republicans, Lincoln did not welcome this eastern interference. Douglas, in defending the principle of popular sovereignty, had continually asserted that it did not matter whether "slavery is voted up or down." This indifference and the principle behind it, Lincoln believed, were immoral. He considered popular sovereignty, under this ad hoc definition, a temporary expedient at best. The nation could not long maintain its precarious balance between the two totally incompatible and emotionally charged social philosophies, and it was therefore in great danger of becoming a citadel of slavery. "Friends," he explained to the committee for his candidacy, "this thing has been retarded long enough. The time has come when these sentiments should be uttered, and if it is decreed that I should go down [because of them] then let me go down linked to the truth."

He "uttered these sentiments" in his first speech as the Republican candidate, predicting that a "'house divided against itself cannot stand.' I believe this government cannot endure permanently half slave and half free. I do not expect the Union to be dissolved—I do not expect the house to fall—but I do expect that it will cease to be divided. It will become all one thing or all the other." This "damned fool utterance," as one of his chagrined supporters described it, would be his major theme in the campaign. It was not a very comfortable thing for his audiences to hear, with its gloomy premonition of confrontation. Douglas was easier to listen to, with his cheery faith in compromise, although this faith was marred by inconsistency, since his principle of popular sovereignty could hardly live side by side with his support for the Dred Scott decision. For all of Lincoln's efforts, the inconsistency seems, by and large, to have been wishfully overlooked.

Douglas did not underestimate Lincoln as an opponent, considering him "the strong man of his party, the best stump speaker in the West." Indeed, he admired him as a man. "Of all the damned Whig rascals about Springfield," he remarked (ignoring the death rattle of the Whig party), "Abe Lincoln is the ablest and most honest." But he was never shy about carrying the implication of Lincoln's position to its bellicose extremes: "Mr. Lincoln advocates boldly and clearly a war of sections, a war of the North against the South, of the free states against the slave states, a war of extermination to be continued relentlessly until the one or the other shall be subdued, and all the states shall either become slave or become free."

The argument, together with many others, continued throughout the summer and early fall in what came to be called The Great Debates. These seven forensic clashes kept the two men traveling and talking up and down the long state, which ranges from a point farther north than New Haven, Connecticut, to another farther south than Richmond, Virginia, and which included regional differences very like those dividing the country as a whole. These collisions "between the Tall Sucker and the Little Giant" held the interest of great crowds of Illinois voters and attracted national attention. Millions of readers could follow the debates in newspapers throughout the land. Lincoln was heartened by this, since part of his purpose was to thwart Douglas's ambition to be elected the country's President in 1860. He therefore sought to exploit the ambiguity of Douglas's position by pressing him to explain how any territory could halt the spread of slavery under the Dred Scot decision. Douglas squirmed evasively for a while but finally, under Lincoln's dogged questioning, suggested that a territorial legislature could effectively bar slavery simply by failing to pass laws protecting it within the territory's borders. This weaseling answer may have won him a little support or perhaps greater tolerance in the North, but it evidently killed him in the deep and dedicated South. Lincoln did what he could to widen the breach, using the sharpest tools in his stump-speaker's kit. His speeches, the *Louisville Journal* reported, were "searching, scathing, stunning. They belong to what someone has graphically styled the *tomahawking* species."

There were other issues in the campaign—the country was still mired in an economic depression that had begun the year before— but Lincoln kept the focus of the debates on the question of freedom. "That is the issue that will continue in this country when these poor tongues of Judge Douglas and myself shall be silent. It is the eternal struggle between these two principles. . . . The one is the common right of humanity and the other the divine right of kings. [The latter is the] spirit that says, 'You work and toil and earn bread, and I'll eat it.' No matter in what shape it comes, whether from the mouth of a king who seeks to bestride the people of his own nation and live by the fruit of their labor, or from one race of men as an apology for enslaving another race, it is the same tyrannical principle."

November 2 was Election Day. Ironically, Douglas was re-elected not because of popular sovereignty—Lincoln received a majority of the popular vote by a margin of some 4,000—but because the voting districts were gerrymandered in his favor, giving southern Illinois an electoral preponderance over the north. In a letter Lincoln's friend and partner William Herndon ascribed the defeat to a failure to equivocate, to "play politics" with the overriding issue: "Lincoln tried to stand high and elevated, so he fell deep." Lincoln himself felt that he failed to do better because Douglas was supported by diverse politicians who expected Douglas to promote their special interests.

Whatever the explanations, he was mightily discouraged. He had been through three months or more of exciting controversy, of severe demands on him both physically and mentally, of unremitting train rides and jostling crowds and noisy parades and aggressive reporters. He had made a prodigious effort and had been found wanting. Whatever the explanations, the defeat was embarrassing and disheartening. And impoverishing. "I have been on expenses so long without earning anything," he wrote to one of the politicians on his election committee, "that I am absolutely without money now even for household purposes." Although he was glad that he had made the race for the hearing it gave his views, he expected personally to "sink out of view" and "be forgotten." The sting of the defeat brought from him his most memorable reaction, the comparison with the boy who had stubbed his toe: "It hurt too bad to laugh, and he was too big to cry." As for any future elections, he promised in another letter that he would be "in no one's way for any of the places." Some days were worse than others. A friend later described visiting him and finding him utterly downcast: "I never saw a man so depressed. I tried to rally his drooping spirits. He was simply steeped in gloom."

In late November 1858, within weeks after the election, three Illinois newspapers recommended the nomination in 1860 of Abraham Lincoln as the Republican candidate for President.

# Ulysses S. Grant and Civilian Life

Ulysses S. Grant hated army life. And he loved his wife, devotedly. The idea of being separated from his wife for the army's sake was more than he could stomach.

Julia Dent of St. Louis was the only woman in his life, and all he ever needed. He was a private, rather withdrawn man who needed a deep, intimate, affectionate, caring relationship with another human being. She provided that relationship. She was the necessary and sufficient condition for his psychological well-being, a glowing light for his darkest days. Later in his career his associates, when they became anxious about his behavior, would call on her for therapy. As long as she was with him, he would be just fine.

He married her in 1848, on his return from the distasteful war with Mexico, in which he had distinguished himself as a soldier despite his opposition to it. They settled into the dreary social rounds of peacetime army life at various posts in the Great Lakes region. Lieutenant Grant disliked the life but was preoccupied with his wife and family (two children by 1852). His state seemed to be one of precarious contentment.

Precarious it was. In the spring of 1852 he was ordered with his outfit, the 4th U.S. Infantry, to the Oregon wilderness. (Having proved himself a splendid horseman at West Point, he naturally was assigned to the infantry.) Although he and Julia dreaded the separation, they agreed that she and the children could not possibly make the trip. Instead, they would have to live with his family in Ohio until, somehow, he could send for them. In later years a fellow officer wrote touchingly of Grant's wistfulness over being separated from his wife and children, although the trip from New York down the east coast, across the Isthmus of Panama, and up the west coast to the Columbia River was such an ordeal (a third of the party died) that he never regretted their decision.

His job as regimental quartermaster kept him frantically busy during the trip, but his work at Fort Vancouver became more routine soon after their arrival. It quickly dawned on him that he could not possibly support his family on his army pay, since the gold rush had brought on a fever of inflation throughout the far west. Moonlighting was the only answer, he decided. The area was booming economically, at least in fits and starts. With a little luck and a lot of free enterprise he had reason to expect enough extra income to keep his family at least in the style to which they were accustomed. To this end he displayed plenty of individual enterprise—but not much luck.

First he went into the potato business with some other enterprising officers. Food prices were so astronomical and potatoes were so popular that growing and marketing that vegetable seemed a sure thing. The industrious group rented some land by the river and farmed it—only to watch helplessly one day while the swollen river washed over their crop and ruined most of it. Their only consolation was that so many others had caught the potato bug in the drive for the fast buck that a potato glut had driven prices down steeply, canceling any profit that Grant & Co. might have realized.

Then another promising market beckoned. San Franciscans needed ice, and the Columbia River had an oversupply. This was indeed a land of opportunity. Grant joined a group to underwrite the shipment of a hundred tons of ice to the city, but the cargo schooner ran into headwinds and arrived much later than its schedule called for. A day or so before its arrival several shiploads of ice had come in from Alaska, and now no one in San Francisco wanted any more ice at any price.

The same sort of thing happened with a hog project. Grant and a friend purchased some hogs from neighboring settlers and shipped them to San Francisco just as the bottom was dropping out of the hog market. They next tried the same thing with chickens. The market held up, but the chickens caught something on the schooner and all died before delivery. On a visit to San Francisco, Grant and some others discovered a ready market for a small recreation complex—a game room offering such pastimes as billiards to the city's burgeoning population of single males. They also found a vacant rooming house readily adaptable to this role and hired a man to operate the establishment during their tours of duty. They gave him the money to make the necessary changes to the house and to buy the equipment, and returned to Fort Vancouver. And never saw him again.

These unremitting if minor disasters at least tended to keep Lieutenant Grant's mind off the army and his loneliness for Julia. But now, with a promotion to captain, he was transferred to Humboldt Bay on the northern California coast and assigned to a line outfit. His duties as quartermaster had held some interest for him, but his duties as a line officer added up to sheer tedium. Worse still, he could find no opportunities for extracurricular activities. Homesickness overcame him, and in his frustration he turned to alcohol. He had plenty of company, of course; army officers on duty in the antipodes have never been known as fervent teetotalers.

His problem was not so much excessive quantity as inadequate capacity. Since he could not hold his liquor, his relatively moderate drinking had conspicuous effects on his behavior. This was especially unfortunate because his commanding officer, a martinet, disliked him for his negligent attitude toward spit and polish. Although the details of this confrontation are historically unclear, evidently the C.O. made an issue of Grant's tippling, insisting that he resign or be formally charged with misconduct. Although Grant almost certainly would have been acquitted by a court martial, he feared that a trial might be just one more thing to come between him and Julia. And, of course, he had had the army up to the earlobes. So he resigned. After the long return trip he arrived in New York penniless, but a draft from his father reached him in time to pay his hotel bill and other debts and get him to Ohio. It was now spring of 1854.

Soon he and Julia and the children moved to some farmland near St. Louis, settling on a sixty-acre spread that Julia had been given by her father. His first chore was to clear away the timber, which he sold on the streets of St. Louis. This role of shabby peddler was painful for him, since he often met old army buddies in the city, and he was a sensitive man. But he kept at it doggedly, conscientiously. After all, he and Julia were together again. And he was not drinking.

For the next two years he worked incessantly to make the farm pay. After building a small house for his family he planted a crop—which he harvested just in time for the farm depression of 1857. The crop was unmarketable. He planted again, but June 1858 brought a record cold that killed the crop and made him so ill that it took him the next six months to recover. Early in 1859, weak and thoroughly discouraged, he sold the farm and moved with his family to St. Louis, where he joined a real estate firm. He quickly learned that he had no talent as a salesman and rent collector, since he regularly paid out in expenses more than he earned in commissions. He applied for a job as an engineer for the county and was rejected. Then the purchaser of his farm announced that he could no longer continue his installment payments, leaving Grant without any income. A job in a customshouse rescued him until a newly appointed customs collector arrived and dismissed the whole staff only a few weeks after Grant had been hired.

That did it. For Grant, appealing to his father for a job was hitting bottom, but he could see no alternative. And so he wound up as a clerk in his father's leather store in Galena, Illinois. However many cuts below his former rank this job may have been on the social pyramid, he apparently did not consider it demeaning—as Robert E. Lee would discover at Appomattox, Grant was never much given to "side." Yet neither did he find it very challenging or fulfilling. For Julia's sake, however, and with her quiet support and companionship, he stuck it out. Meanwhile he worried over the fate of the Union, which seemed on the brink of dissolution. He was no abolitionist, although he had freed the one slave he ever owned at a time when he desperately needed the thousand dollars that a sale would have netted him. But he was a fervent unionist. After the bombardment of Fort Sumter and Lincoln's call for volunteers, he presided at a mass meeting held in Galena in response to that call. Ever diffident, he refused the command of several volunteer regiments (by election). He did apply to the War Department for a regular regimental command (by appointment) but never received an answer (his letter was found some years later, apparently unread). He applied to Major General George B. McClellan, an old army acquaintance and a comer by all accounts, but George was too busy, or something, to see him. He also applied to an old West Point friend, now the commander at St. Louis, but got no response. It looked more and more as though he would spend the war in the leather store.

Then Richard Yates, the governor of Illinois, suddenly found himself saddled with a volunteer regiment that was about to go out of business. The men had signed up for thirty days but, as the end of that duty approached, were now about to be asked to volunteer for the full three-year stretch. They had lost all discipline, however, under the command of a thoroughly inept regimental colonel. Yates, warned by a friend that Grant preferred duty in the regular army and in any case was too diffident to present himself as a solution to Yates's problem, simply appointed Grant to the position of colonel and told him to whip the hellions into shape.

Grant obeyed, taking command in June 1861, without a uniform and looking not much more imposing than he had looked as a wood peddler. But he transformed the regiment.

Two months later he was promoted to brigadier general. And he did not spend the war in the leather store.

# Fyodor Dostoevsky and the Roulette Tables

F yodor Dostoevsky knew failure, of one sort or another, throughout most of his adult life. As a young man he was sentenced to death for engaging in a political conspiracy. He had already mounted the scaffold when word came of a reprieve. Under his reduced sentence he served four years of hard labor in Siberia and then four more similarly miserable years as a dogface in the Russian army. This was followed by poverty-stricken years of struggling to continue his writing despite the importunate demands of parasitical relatives, the fraudulent tactics of unscrupulous publishers, the ceaseless nagging of countless creditors, and his own helplessness in handling money—all aggravated by continual attacks of his chronic epilepsy. Although his first novel, *Poor Folk*, published in 1846 when he was only twenty-five, was critically acclaimed, his work over the next twenty years met with reactions ranging from indifference to antagonism. How much of this can appropriately be called "failure" may be debatable, but his life, in any conventional sense, was hardly one of undiluted success.

His most spectacular failure was not a literary one, although it interfered with his literary efforts. This was his inability to overcome his severe addiction to gambling, reflected in his heavily autobiographical short novel, *The Gambler.* Since it was a failure due to a defect in his character, to an ingrained flaw, self-help seems to have been out of the question. He could be helped only by another, and the story of his rescue through the undemanding love and commonsensical solicitude of another is as spectacular as the story of his failure.

In 1866 he published *Crime and Punishment,* but it would be years before the novel would bring him any substantial praise or money. His desperate circumstances had forced him into signing an incredible contract with a publisher named Stelovsky. If he failed to submit a new novel to Stelovsky by November 1 of that year, all rights to his publications, past and future, would thereafter be held by the publisher. In September he began having trouble with his eyes and an occulist, warning him that he could go blind if he did not ease up, recommended that he dictate his work instead of writing it out. The director of a shorthand college in the vicinity (this was in St. Petersburg) had just the person to help him: his best pupil, one Anna Snitkina.

It was a choice fortuitous beyond belief. Her parents apparently had been omnivorous readers (her father had died shortly before this) and had liked Dostoevsky's stories so much that they had nicknamed Anna "Netochka" after one of his characters. Anna herself was an ardent fan and now was enraptured by the thought of helping out her idol. At their first session Dostoevsky, who had had an epileptic seizure the night before, was unwell and in a foul mood. He dictated dictatorially, demanding that she read everything back, complaining that she was too slow and made too many errors, and in the end dismissing her peremptorily—yet telling her to return the next day at the same time. Anna went home furious, fully resolved never to see that unbearable tyrant again.

The next morning, however, she relented and, conscientious girl that she was, went back for more.

During the following three or four weeks the writer and his stenographer evidently produced enough to satisfy the terms of the Stelovsky contract, in quantity if not in quality. More important for them both, Dostoevsky had shown himself in some of his better moods, and a bond of affection was developing between them. Indeed, Anna, utterly fascinated by this mercurial genius, had fallen hopelessly in love. Her sister emphasized the "hopelessly" to her: Anna was twenty and he was forty-four, penniless, debt-ridden, ill, and thoroughly unreliable. What neither sister knew was that Dostoevsky, since the death of his first wife, a harpy, some thirty months earlier, had already proposed marriage to four other women. But knowing this would have made no more difference to Anna than did her sister's warning. It was too late for hesitation. When Dostoevsky proposed obliquely, symbolically, telling her that he had found an unexpected diamond buried among his manuscripts, she accepted radiantly. They were married in February 1867.

The first weeks of marriage were cruel ones for Anna chiefly because of mistreatment from Dostoevsky's stepson and sister-in-law, who seem to have resembled Cinderella's older sisters. Anna's mother, who had not strongly opposed the marriage but was now having very sober second thoughts, urged her daughter to take a trip outside the country with her husband, so that she could have these precious early weeks with him away from relatives. She could underwrite some of the expense, and Anna could sell or pawn some of her clothes and furniture and other belongings. Anna, after doing so, proposed the trip to Dostoevsky. Well, yes, he responded reluctantly, we can go—but only for two or three months. They left shortly before Easter, and they would not return for more than four years.

The next four months were the nadir. Dostoevsky did no writing at all. The only writing was done by Anna, who, to the later delight of her husband's biographers, kept a meticulous diary—in shorthand, simply to keep in practice. The newlyweds' first stop was Dresden. In mid-May Dostoevsky left her there to pay a visit to Hamburg's roulette tables. He would be gone only four days, he assured her, and would return with enough money for them to pay all his debts and travel through Europe in style. She let him go reluctantly, though without protest. It was his dream, she wrote in her diary; to deny its fulfillment would rob him of all peace.

About a week later she received a letter from him. He had lost all the money that he had taken with him—would she please send him some of the money that he had left with her? Although being alone in a strange city made her miserable, she sent him the money and told him not to hurry back. He didn't. It took him ten days to lose the money, then to pawn his watch and lose *that* money. On the eleventh day he appeared in Dresden, pockets empty. Anna was deliriously happy at his return, although he had lost all the money that had been intended to last them through the year.

An appeal to her mother brought them something to get by on while Dostoevsky begged an advance—indeed, a second advance—from a publisher named Katkov, for whom he was ostensibly writing a book and from whom, astonishingly, he now received eighty-four gold napoleons (and a note to the effect that there would be no more advances). After paying their bills, the couple left Dresden on Thursday morning, July 4, arriving in Baden-Baden that evening. The day's trip was a hot, dirty train ride and was especially hard on Anna, who was suffering from morning sickness. They had sixty-five napoleons. And Baden-Baden, unfortunately, was a veritable Monte Carlo.

Next morning Dostoevsky took fifteen napoleons to a nearby casino and quickly lost them all at roulette. Crestfallen, he agreed with Anna, who theoretically controlled the family purse, that he should visit the casino not more often than once a day. That afternoon, however, he persuaded Anna that he wanted to show her the casino, and on their visit he lost another five napoleons.

On the next morning Anna fell ill, and Dostoevsky offered to stay with her and be of whatever help he could. Although she eagerly accepted his offer, he shortly thereafter excused himself to make a half-hour visit to the casino. After losing twenty napoleons at the tables he returned home, thoroughly depressed, at eleven that evening. The next day, Sunday the seventh, since Anna was feeling better, Dostoevsky felt free to leave in the morning with five napoleons. Soon he was back, abjectly apologetic but not too contrite to forego a return to the casino with two more napoleons. He came home again, and left again, three more times. When he reappeared for the last time at the end of the day, there were only a dozen napoleons left in the family purse.

During that week Dostoevsky's luck changed radically from disastrous to respectable. His good fortune continued through Tuesday the sixteenth; that evening he and Anna counted no less than 166 napoleons in the purse. Anna begged him to make arrangements to leave Baden-Baden the next morning. But there is no more compulsive gambler than a winning compulsive gambler, and by Wednesday night the family fortune had shrunk to 20 napoleons. On Thursday he gambled away 19 of these and then pawned a pair of earrings and a brooch that he had given Anna after their wedding. They netted him 6 napoleons, which he promptly lost at the tables. On Friday the nineteenth he took the last napoleon and all the small change in the house, pawned their wedding rings, parlayed the proceeds up to 180 francs, lost 177, ran a winning streak up to 180 again, redeemed the rings, and returned triumphantly to Anna. She paid the overdue rent.

By the end of July the Dostoevskys were utterly destitute again and on the verge of being evicted for nonpayment of rent. One day near the end of the month he had sold her fur coat for eight francs, leaving her two francs for dinner; after losing the six francs, he had returned, taken the two francs, and lost them as well. On another day he had sold a couple of her dresses and speedily lost the thirty francs that they had brought. The month of August introduced no change, except in the form of some money from Anna's sympathetic mother and sister, accompanied by a note from her mother reporting that time had run out on Anna's pawned furniture, which the pawnbroker would now try to sell. Dostoevsky gambled away the money and dismissed the loss of the furniture with a mild oath. Finally, after three miserable weeks of precarious skimping and borrowing, Anna managed somehow to persuade her husband that they should go to Switzerland as originally, and somewhat vaguely, planned. They left on August 23, arriving in Geneva with a total of eighteen francs. And he began writing again, on the first chapters of *The Idiot*.

In Geneva Anna had a radical idea. She knew that her husband had been a compulsive gambler for many years despite the severe disapproval and remonstrances of those around him. This opposition, she suspected, would probably aggravate, rather than lessen, any compulsion in such a congenital maverick. Suppose someone were to encourage him to gamble—would he begin to lose the urge?

So she suggested that he try his luck at the roulette tables in nearby Aix-les-Bains. Since you should never expect to win in the long run, she urged, take only a specific amount and stop when it's gone. He tried it and it worked. He came home that day with his nongambling reserve still intact, and he got back to work. He suffered a serious relapse in the spring of 1868, brought on perhaps by the death of his beloved infant daughter at the age of ten weeks, but recovered quickly enough for it not to affect his writing.

As the couple resumed their leisurely tour of Europe, Anna would occasionally urge him to try the roulette tables, always with their mutually determined limit. He did so, but apparently with waning absorption. In April 1871, on their way back to Russia, she recommended the tables at Wiesbaden. He lost some money there, but his heart did not seem to be in it. Indeed, he was preoccupied with ideas about the characters who were to people his immortal *The Brothers Karamazov*.

After that day he never gambled again.

# Paul Cézanne and the Fogies

In Paris the 1860s were a time of artistic ferment. The advancement of the physical sciences, especially optics, had entered into artistic studies of light and color, and many young painters were excitedly experimenting with unprecedented methods for achieving unprecedented effects. The artistic establishment, accustomed to the realistic compositions of what art historians today call the neoclassicism, romanticism, and naturalism of the early nineteenth century, had the customary attitude of settled conservatives toward the unprecedented.

During the sixties, however, they suffered occasional attacks of mild liberality. In this weakened condition they sometimes issued restrained invitations to a few of the young radicals to enter some of their works in the official Salons' annual exhibitions. The Salon juries could be tolerant as long as these few paintings could be hung unobtrusively amid a vast thicket of more conventional works, but by 1870 the jury members had become uneasily aware of something like a population explosion in bohemia. Rather than show the new art in representative numbers, the juries of the seventies closed the doors of the Salons to anyone without long-standing conservative credentials.

As a result, most of the frustrated outcasts stopped submitting paintings for the Salon exhibitions and formed their own society for annual showings of unconventional art. One of the exceptions was Paul Cézanne, who, although a member of the new group, continued to send in samples of his work for Salon exhibitions in what seems an almost masochistic yearning for annual rejection. The man who has been called the father of modern art, whose paintings were indeed generally more revolutionary than those of his radical colleagues, was personally less rebellious than his dissident peers and less noisily defiant of the authority wielded by the traditionalists. He wanted recognition from on high without the knuckling-under that such recognition demanded.

In mid-April of 1874 the group hired some rooms on a busy boulevard, collected works from thirty artists, and for the next four weeks kept their makeshift gallery open for the delectation of passersby and other visitors. The exhibition soon attracted a great deal of attention from a great many visitors, including art critics. But the public attention was overwhelmingly unflattering, ranging from bursts of high dudgeon to waves of derisive guffaws. The critics' reactions similarly ranged from shocked fulmination to acid satire. In the latter category was a waggish review by one Louis Leroy which introduced the label of "Impressionism" to cover most of the works being shown. Leroy told of accompanying a traditional painter to the gallery, where his friend was so profoundly impressed with the radical artists' impressions of nature and their other subjects that he went berserk. Everything and everyone in the gallery became merely an "impression" for him, and as he and the critic departed he criticized the doorman, who had sharply recognizable features instead of smudges, as the work of some stuffy academician. The review was entitled "L'Exposition des Impressionistes."

The three Cézanne paintings included in the exhibit—Cézanne was considered, and considered himself, an impressionist at the time, though not in his later years—came in for especially harsh criticism. Even a relatively liberal critic, one who had expressed some quiet admiration for paintings by Claude Monet, Edgar Degas, and Pierre Renoir, waxed quite nasty in his comments on Cézanne's. The two landscapes he found intolerably audacious, simply too much to swallow. As for the third entry, A Modern Olympia, a trancelike rendition of Manet's famous Olympia, the review described it as inviting public derision and revealing its creator to be insane or at least suffering from delirium tremens whenever he tried to apply paint to canvas.

When the exhibition closed Cézanne returned to his home in Aix-en-Provence, northeast of Marseilles, and resumed his painting with more equanimity than most artists could have displayed after such a reception of their work. But he was a patient man, confident in the eventual recognition of his talent. In addition, he had an easy sense of humor useful for cushioning the heaviest blows. In June he wrote Camille Pissarro that he had just had a visit from the director of the Aix museum, who confessed that he had been rather unnerved by the reports of the radicals' Paris exhibition and had decided to visit Cézanne's studio to see how great the peril to good painting might be. "But when I told him that viewing my works would give him only a limited notion of how far the evil had gone, and that he really should see the true criminals' work in Paris, he reassured me, 'I'll be able to get some idea of the hazards to painting by taking a look at your offenses.'" Cézanne responded to this candor with a good-natured effort to explain what he was trying to accomplish in his paintings, the director's anxiety abated, and the two men parted on excellent terms.

The radical group, after skipping a year, opened their next exhibition in Paris in mid-April 1876. They had accepted the "impressionist" label and were already in the process of hardening their views into a new orthodoxy. As a result, the group of thirty painters represented in the 1874 show had shaken down to a leaner, more homogeneous group of nineteen. Cézanne failed to submit any entries, for some reason now lost in the mists of history, perhaps because the exhibition was held in a gallery lent by a sympathetic private art dealer rather than in one rented for the purpose, and he may have found this demeaning. He remained on good terms with the impressionists, however, as became clear the next year.

The exhibition in the spring of 1877 included sixteen of Cézanne's canvases, prominently displayed on a wall generally considered to be the most desirable position in the gallery. The public reaction to the exhibition as a whole was less derisive, more sympathetic, than it had been three years earlier, especially toward the less radical departures from the comfortably familiar. The greater sympathy may have been due partly to the persistent educational campaign informally conducted in the gallery, day after day, by a collector of modest means but great enthusiasm, a minor customs official named Victor Choquet whose favorite painter was none other than Paul Cézanne. Despite his limited success in softening public hostility, he could not extend that success to Cézanne, who again wound up as the butt of the public's and the critics' displeasure. One critic described his work as almost unimaginable, as laughable but lamentable, and as exhibiting an ignorance of composition and color that one ordinarily associates with children. Nor could Choquet, who had bought several of Cézanne's paintings, persuade any other collectors to buy a single canvas. The impressionists' works generally could be sold for ridiculously low prices, often at humiliating auctions, but Cézanne's (except for Choquet) could not be sold, period.

The patient optimism that he had shown before may have deserted him at this point, at least for a time. He returned to Aix and continued to paint—and to submit a painting each year to the Salons, a habit that even he considered a forlorn exercise in total futility. He withdrew into a solitude broken only by occasional visits from his closest friends—Choquet, Pissarro, Monet, Renoir, and Emile Zola—and was quite forgotten by the public and the critics. He submitted no further canvases for exhibition, and his work did not appear in Paris again until 1895, and then rather unsuccessfully. Kept going by an inheritance, he never stopped painting, and in 1899 finally was included in a Salon exhibition. At last both the critics and the public were ready for him. Thereafter his paintings were actually in demand. By the time of his death in 1906, he could feel that his patience had been justified.

# Georges Bizet and
## *Carmen*

In the fall of 1874 the Opéra-Comique theater in Paris was owned and operated by an impresario named Camille du Locle, and he was having a rather bad time of it. The theater had been slowly but painfully losing audiences and money for the past three years. During 1874 it had barely escaped going under, being saved chiefly by a succession of SRO performances at which Verdi conducted his *Requiem Mass*. The irony in this rescue was noted by a critic who observed that it had required a mass for the dead to restore the Opéra-Comique to life.

Du Locle was very nervous about the prospects for 1875. He had recently commissioned the rising young composer Georges Bizet to write a new opera. Rehearsals had begun earlier that fall, and du Locle was dismayed by both the libretto and the music. He dreaded presenting this vulgar stew to discriminating Parisian audiences in the spring, but he was committed, especially since it was too late now to come up with any practical alternative. So he vented his frustration in caustic comments on the work addressed not only to Bizet but also to the librettist (Ludovic Halévy), the singers, the stagehands, whoever happened to be within hearing range. The music, he fumed, was "Cochin-Chinese" and completely unintelligible.

The complaints did nothing to boost the morale of the company, who were themselves uneasy over the difficulty of the score, the unprecedented demands of the libretto for naturalistic, uninhibited acting not only from the principals but even from the chorus, and the unfamiliarity of the plebeian setting. On the last point, for instance, the girls employed in the cigarette factory were expected to smoke cigarettes on stage while behaving like hoydens, and this created considerable consternation, expressed chiefly in much raucous coughing during rehearsals of the scene. Du Locle's barbs acutely aggravated the tension. If he had been eager to ensure the opera's failure, he could hardly have made a greater contribution.

Bizet was taut with anxiety, since he considered the opera decisive for his career. *His* tension was aggravated also by persistent demands for changes from du Locle and others. The orchestra insisted that the music must be simplified, that as it stood it simply could not be played; Bizet in response insisted on several extra rehearsals, which persuaded the orchestra members that the music could be played after all. When du Locle demanded that the ending be changed and Bizet refused, the director of the Comédie-Francaise was called in to arbitrate the dispute. He seemed to consider the dispute irrelevant, since he found the whole opera repulsive, predicting that, whatever the ending, it would fail ignominiously and would ruin the theater's reputation as well as Bizet's. Daunted by such comments, Bizet frantically made changes throughout the opera, rewriting Carmen's opening song, the famous "Habanera," more than a dozen times.

Opening night was scheduled for March 3, 1875. In February Bizet was awarded the Cross of the Legion of Honor, but the decoration came too late to act as much of a tranquilizer. He may well have been aware of the rumor that it had been presented before the premiere lest the quality of the opera make a subsequent award ridiculous. And he certainly was aware that nothing so minor as a Legion of Honor ribbon could protect him from the slings and arrows of predatory hordes of critics expected to descend on the theater that evening.

Finally the dreaded evening arrived. The first act went well, eliciting some applause for the "Habanera" and the love duet and, at the end, some curtain calls for the cast. During the first intermission well-wishers filled the stage to congratulate Bizet and all the others involved in the production. In the opening of the second act the "Toreador Song" (which Bizet himself considered crowd-pleasing "ordure") drew great applause, but from this point on everything went downhill as the opera departed increasingly from the conventions of its time. At the end of the act the applause was more perfunctory, and during the intermission only a few people were on stage—and during the third intermission still fewer, so few indeed that Bizet slipped outside and paced about with his publisher, bemoaning the miserable flop he had produced. Friends came out to cheer him up, but he was inconsolable.

With three or four exceptions the reviews, which appeared in various papers during the next few days, were devastating. Some critics were deeply offended, at least ostensibly, by the sympathetic musical portrayal of a thoroughly wanton woman, "a wild woman, part savage and part Andalusian, sensual and insolent, without shame, believing in neither God nor Satan"—"truly a gutter whore." Other operas had included courtesans and faithless women, but never so brazen a baggage as this! One particularly outraged reviewer suggested that Carmen ought to be gagged, have a flagon of cold water poured over her, and be put in a straitjacket to stop her hip-wiggling. How this would have furthered the action he did not say, and he left open the question of who most needed a cold shower.

Others, less prurient, held forth on the dramatic and musical shortcomings, ranging from unbearable to intolerable. The score, one wrote, did have some recognizable themes, but they were stale and undistinguished. The opera had no unity, no perceptible plan, no scenic or dramatic quality. The music was dissonant and dryly academic, lacking natural vigor and devoid of melody. (Yes, devoid of melody!) Traditionalists condemned it as too Wagnerian while Wagnerians condemned it as too traditionalist (it did fall between the two schools in this respect). It was contrasted most unfavorably with the immortal music of composers like Auber, Adam, Hérold, and Boieldieu.

Bizet surely would have been less vulnerable to this critical vitriol if the opera had been a financial success, showing some evidence of its popular appeal. Although it was performed forty-five times that year at the Opéra-Comique, it consistently played to half-empty, sometimes almost completely empty, houses. Toward the end of its run du Locle was giving away free tickets by the bundle. It may be that he had tapped a hidden reservoir of loyalty to Bizet, but in all probability he kept on showing the opera because he had no real choice. Thus the sensitive Bizet was confronted for weeks with evidence, as he saw it, that vindicated the critics. It might well have been easier on him if the show had folded quietly after the first performance.

A few days after the premiere a good friend of Bizet's, meeting the composer on the street, was appalled by his look of severe depression. Having attended the second performance, when the audience had shown greater enthusiasm, he described its reaction to Bizet in terms as glowing as he could make them. Bizet listened attentively but rather grimly, responding at last with a bitter allusion to the disastrous reviews. The friend, who before had often seen Bizet engaging excitedly in spirited argument, tried desperately to arouse him now from his alarming apathy. He condemned the critics loudly, vehemently, in the hope of striking a spark of anger, but Bizet only listened impassively, occasionally pressing his friend's hand in a show of grateful understanding. Eventually he ended the conversation with a deeply weary shrug, sighing, "Ah, maybe they're right."

A couple of weeks later he suffered from a severe flare-up of a throat ulcer that had often troubled him before. His recoveries in the past had always been rapid. But this time he was too weak, too dispirited. "You wouldn't believe how old I feel," he remarked to a visitor. (He was thirty-seven.) About two months later, by early June, he was dead. *Carmen* was still playing to a nearly empty house.

The three or four favorable reviews had never been enough to console him. But it seems especially unfortunate that he died too soon to read Tchaikovsky's prophetic comment, written in the winter of 1875–1876 (and quoted by Herbert Weinstock in his biography *Tchaikovsky*): "*Carmen* is a masterpiece in every sense. . . . I am convinced that within ten years *Carmen* will be the most popular opera in the whole world."

# Mohandas Gandhi and the Practice of Law

As a boy Mohandas Gandhi, according to one of his biographers, Louis Fischer, "seemed to have little ability and less talent." In his sixties Gandhi himself wrote in his autobiography that about all he could recall of his schooling was "getting through" the multiplication tables with difficulty, avoiding any reading beyond school texts, and emulating his classmates in calling their teacher "all kinds of names." In addition, he was excruciatingly shy: "To be at school at the stroke of the hour, and to run back home as soon as the school closed—that was my daily habit. I literally ran back, because I could not bear to talk to anybody. I was even afraid lest anyone should poke fun at me." Astonishing diffidence, this, in one who was later to face down nothing less than the British Empire.

His experience in London as a young man did little to reassure him. At the age of eighteen, almost nineteen, he was sent there by members of his extended family for a law degree, which could be obtained in a three-year crash course. Still anxious lest anyone poke fun at him, he became distracted by his need, and his efforts, to appear an English gentleman. Evening clothes, a "chimney-pot hat," double gold watch chain, enervating struggles with unruly hair, long and close encounters with the mirror—these were the matters that preoccupied him. He took lessons in elocution, in dancing, in the violin, failing at each so miserably that he finally turned in desperation to his law studies, eager to get them over with so that he could return to India. Thus motivated, he did manage to achieve the formal status of barrister in June 1891, and on the very next day he left England.

That particular status should have done him more good than it did. It would have, if he had had any talent for the law as it was practiced in India. As a barrister, a lawyer trained in England, he ranked well about the *vakils*, which is what the lawyers trained in India were called. He found Indian law tedious and its legal procedures quite impenetrable. In addition, he rigidly refused to pay a tout a commission for bringing him a case, although this was the universal practice among lawyers at all levels for reasons of survival. He received a great deal of stern advice concerning this attitude, which his advisers considered tantamount to a starvation wish.

He finally did get one case, for the Small Causes Court in Bombay. Although it was a simple civil suit, he had to plead for the defendant in court, and this meant cross-examining the plaintiff's witnesses. When the time came, Gandhi recounted, "I rose, but my heart sank into my shoes." He stood there for a few moments, trying desperately to summon up some composure, and indeed even to summon up a question. "My head was spinning and I felt as though the whole court was doing the same." Sinking abjectly into his chair, he informed his client that he could not go on, recommended another lawyer, and returned his fee. Later the other lawyer, engaged for almost twice Gandhi's fee, won the case easily.

That was the end—in fact, it was the beginning, the middle, and the end—of his career as a trial lawyer. One other case came his way during six-month stay in Bombay, the preparation of a brief for a poor farmer whose land had been confiscated. No fee. Desperately, Gandhi cast about for some other way to make a living.

He came across a help wanted ad in a newspaper: "Wanted: an English teacher to teach one hour daily." His English was quite good, and the ad was from a very reputable, even celebrated Bombay high school. He eagerly wrote a letter of application, mailed it, and was called in for an interview. But when the principal realized that Gandhi did not have a conventional college degree, he immediately lost interest. Gandhi protested that his command of English was fortified and enhanced by his understanding of Latin, but the principal was adamant. No degree, no place for you here, my dear fellow.

Gandhi was, by his own later account, "in despair." After discussing his predicament with his elder brother, who was a *vakil*, a "petty pleader," in their home town of Rajkot some 250 miles to the northwest, he sadly concluded that he was wasting time in Bombay. His time there had yielded him nothing but a lesson in the benefits of walking. Avoiding carriages and tramcars for his daily visits to the High Court, he had accustomed himself to making the ninety-minute round trip on foot in the remorseless Indian sun. He would come to appreciate the value of the lesson to his health and to his politics, but not until much later.

His return home was hardly a triumphant one. In the ensuing weeks he managed to eke out a living from performing odd jobs for his brother's modest law partnership. Yet even more demeaning than this awkward situation was a minor but intensely personal encounter he had at this time with British imperialism. In England he had become acquainted with a British civil servant then on leave from India. This man was now back on duty in the colony, holding a post of some political importance. He was in a position to further, or thwart, the political ambitions of Gandhi's elder brother, who unfortunately had somehow antagonized him in an earlier incident. The brother therefore asked Gandhi to pay the official a visit in his behalf. Gandhi resisted. The brother persisted.

Gandhi's feeling of deep obligation to his brother, in addition to a very real affection, finally won, although it went severely against Gandhi's grain to "use his influence," especially in an environment that seemed to prize "influence" above every commodity.

And so, when he had summoned up the courage, he forced himself to make an appointment to see the official. But his visit was a disaster. He was treated not to a warm welcome, but to a cool reception. It soon grew clear that the relationship depended greatly on geography: India was not England. He tried to plead his brother's cause, but the official dismissed his effort with a curt reminder that his brother should go through the proper channels. Gandhi, anxious not to return home with still another failure, continued his appeal. The official asked him to leave. Gandhi went on doggedly promoting his brother's cause. The official, calling on his reserves of native servants, had him forcibly ejected.

Gandhi at first was furious. He wrote the official a note demanding "amends" and threatening to sue him. The official replied in a note accusing Gandhi of intolerable rudeness and challenging him to take whatever action he wished. Gandhi returned to his brother thoroughly crestfallen. The two of them cast about for some practical action to take against the official but gave up the search after a prominent barrister advised them that, if they wished to continue earning any kind of living in that region of India, obsequious discretion would be the better part of impudent valor. "I pocketed the insult," Gandhi wrote in his memoirs, but the "shock changed the course of my life," although at the time his reaction was almost totally a sense of humiliation and bitter failure.

As he continued toiling away at his hack job, he longed for release from the "poisonous atmosphere" of fawning sycophancy that permeated the political and social life of colonial India. When an opportunity came to move to South Africa, therefore, he embraced it hungrily. The offer was from a large firm that needed someone, educated in the law and reasonably fluent in English, to help expedite a long-standing lawsuit. The job would last only a year, or less, and included a respectable fee. And it might even provide a touch of class, which the young Gandhi yearned for more ardently than he ever would in later life. Although the offer meant leaving his wife and two children in the care of his extended family, it was irresistible.

He was quickly disillusioned. South Africa was no more a comfortable place for "colored" people than it is today. His status in Durban, where the firm was headquartered, was that of "coolie barrister," although his intelligence and industry won him the respect of the firm's illiterate but shrewd Arab owner. On a trip from Durban to Pretoria, where the lawsuit was to be tried, he and his luggage were thrown off the train halfway there because he insisted on keeping his seat in the first-class section, since he had a first-class ticket. Tickets were less important than pigmentation, however, and he spent a very cold night in a station in the frigid African highlands without his overcoat. The coat was in his luggage, which the stationmaster had placed in another room, and Gandhi explained "I did not dare to ask for it lest I should be insulted again." In the morning the next train arrived, and he continued his trip at the required class level.

Since the rail line had not been completed all the way to Pretoria, the last part of the trip was by stagecoach. As the only non-white among the travelers, he was required to ride with the driver and a native Hottentot servant up in the coachbox rather than inside with the others. At the first stop, however, a white man, a representative of the stagecoach company, decided that he preferred to sit in the coachbox, to smoke and perhaps to get some fresh air. He ordered Gandhi to sit on the coach footboard. Gandhi, indignantly protesting the injustice of the demand, refused to get down. The man tried to drag him down, and indeed pulled him off the seat, but Gandhi clung to the coachbox railing, clutching it grimly while the man beat him and condemned his insolence in high-decibel blasphemies. But before any bones were broken the other passengers reacted with sympathy for the underdog, arguing with the aggressor that Gandhi should be allowed to continue the trip inside the coach. Although the bully found this suggestion unconscionable, he did relent to the extent of letting Gandhi keep his seat and assigning the Hottentot to the footboard. The trip was completed without further incident.

In Pretoria Gandhi managed to get representatives of the two sides in the lawsuit together and to arrange a compromise sufficiently satisfactory to both and less expensive than carrying the litigation to its bitter end. This, he now found, was where his real legal talent lay, in seeking solutions elsewhere than in court. The discovery was to bring him, at last, some success and satisfaction in the practice of law.

But, more important, a week after the railway and stagecoach incidents, he brought together a group of Indians for a meeting in Pretoria at which he gave a speech on the subject of white discrimination. It was the start of a new career, this speech in 1893. Except for a brief absence in 1896, when he went back to get his family, he was to stay in South Africa for the next twenty-one years. When he returned to India in 1914 his diffidence and sense of failure had long before evaporated, and the British little suspected what he had in store for them.

# Thomas Edison and the "Ogden Baby"

T he really spectacular failure of Thomas Edison's life came not at the beginning of his career but in the middle. An early invention, the electric vote recorder, had failed not technically but commercially because Congress and state legislatures were afraid that it would eliminate the horse trading that could change close votes during the glacial progress of vote tallies. But the device eventually was accepted, and its temporary rejection was barely enough to distract the young Edison from the many other projects requiring his fascinated attention.

The failure of his Ogden mine, however—his "Ogden Baby," as he called it—was anything but peripheral. This huge quarry demanded almost all his attention for nearly a decade (his fascinated attention, as always, for he was a man given to total absorption). It cost him his entire fortune and more, leaving him precariously, if briefly, in debt. It took several lives, almost including his own. And it even came to be known as "Edison's Folly."

The reason for it lay in the economics of the steel industry. After

106

the commercial failure of his vote recorder Edison had vowed never again to try to invent something that nobody wanted. By the 1880s he had invented several things that great multitudes did want. He had greatly improved the telegraph and telephone, had invented a workable phonograph, and had introduced the first practical electric light; such contributions had earned him the title of "The Wizard of Menlo Park." Now he anticipated a growing demand for iron ore from the steel industry, particularly from plants in the east. Midwestern plants had the advantage of rich new ore deposits and cheap water transportation in the Great Lakes region, while eastern mills were beginning to suffer from malnutrition. The richer iron ore mines in the east were too close to being played out to be counted on as a reliable source of usable raw material. The potential mines remaining offered much poorer, less economical types of rock—magnetite, for example, which generally contains less than a third as much iron as hematite. Edison, who as early as 1882 had been deeply impressed by the black magnetite sands that then stretched for miles along the shores of Long Island, felt sure that such rock could be made to yield iron economically. With a little Edison know-how.

In 1889, after the merger of many small electric companies into Edison General Electric had made him a millionaire, he began investing his newly acquired wealth in prospecting extensively for magnetite deposits in Appalachia. One of the most likely areas, his prospectors found, lay near the northern tip of New Jersey, not far from Ogdensburg, where they discovered a veritable mountain of magnetite. Here, he decided, was the site for his grand venture.

The key to the operation was size. After blasting, enormous boulders would be transported from the quarry by enormous steam shovels and enormous cranes and enormous conveyors to enormous rock crushers. The boulders would be crushed into rocks, the rocks into pebbles, the pebbles into gravel, the gravel into sand, and the sand into rock dust. This dust would then be poured through a giant funnel and allowed to fall between powerful electromagnets, which would draw the iron particles into bins ranged down along the path of the dust fall, allowing the rest of the dust to drop to the bottom and be hauled away for sale as construction material. The equipment used for this process, expensive as well as gargantuan, included the biggest steam shovel in the country, shipped in pieces from Chicago where it had been employed in digging the famous drainage canal, and a mobile crane with a span of over 200 feet. The work force soon began rising to its peak of 400 men.

Edison was in his element, solving problems by the carload, overcoming crises, sharing the primitive living conditions and considerable occupational hazards with his hired hands. One serious problem arose early when he found that the final product, the iron oxide powder, was too light to be handled and shipped to the mills without a great deal of it being spilled and carried off by air currents. To eliminate this loss he added a final process in which the powder was formed by heat and pressure, with a viscous binder, into small, transportable bricks. This solved the transportation problem but created severe headaches during the smelting process at the mills. A generally satisfactory answer never was found, although Edison badly needed one to make his product competitive.

Problems abounded every day, with solutions creating new problems. The colossal machinery, subjected to unprecedented stresses and strains as it tried to digest the indigestible, broke down continually, quite literally grinding to a halt. It proved especially sensitive to having steel tools, such as an occasional sledgehammer, dropped inadvertently into its busy maws. The foundation for the 120-ton crushers cracked and the whole assembly tilted out of use. On another occasion the 81-foot-high tower in which the powdered ore was dried clogged up. Edison and the plant superintendent crawled into it through a small opening at the bottom to find out what had gone wrong. Moments later the jam broke and some 30,000 pounds of ground iron ore buried the two men alive. Luckily several workers knew where they were and, after a period of frantic digging, the two men were extracted unharmed.

Edison evidently had underestimated the amount of wear and tear on the equipment or overestimated the equipment's strength and durability, or both. Things wore out faster than anticipated—extractors, conveyors, crushers, even the electromagnets. Weather and insects made working difficult; the unrelenting dust made it almost intolerable. As a result, the turnover in the workforce was even more rapid than in the equipment. Skilled workers were especially hard to hold, and this made the problems in maintaining the machinery all the more intractable. The whole operation was alarmingly inefficient and expensive.

Edison poured money into it. By mid-1892 he had put in $750,000, in addition to $100,000 which had simply disappeared from the disorganized accounts ledgers. That October he carried out a test run to determine whether a number of changes he had made had improved the final product. The raw magnetite had been running about 20 percent iron and his powdered iron bricks, he found, tested at 42 percent. But this was his final product, ready for shipment to the mills. Rich ores like hematite, right out of the ground, contained 70 percent. He was like Alice in Wonderland, hitting his head on an unyielding ceiling, but without a magic cake.

In the winter of 1897–1898 Bethlehem Steel came through with an order for 10,000 tons, large enough to encourage Edison to spend almost a year gearing up the plant to fill it. He got his Ogden Baby operating at top capacity the following winter, pulverizing the gutted mountain and shipping it off to the furnaces in Bethlehem. But the winter was a severe one, interfering with production and increasing costs. It was not only that he was running out of money for his gigantic rat hole. The country was suffering from a major economic depression, and the price of iron ore at the eastern mills had fallen some 40 percent in the past few years. The latest news from the great Mesabi range in Minnesota was that the formidable John D. Rockefeller, among others, had devised cheaper methods (such as specially designed railroad cars) for getting the rich mid-western ores to the eastern mills. And now, for the final blow, Edison was discovering that, as he dug further into his mountain, the magnetite was yielding less and less iron—about half the proportion of the early days—which meant that he would have to process twice as much rock for the same amount of deliverable ore.

Edison's resources, physical as well as financial, were exhausted. One night during that terrible winter—after a day full of fractured gears, conveyors clogged with water-laden sand, tilted elevator towers, burnt-out bearings, snapped cables, and frozen men and machinery—he arrived at his hut from work so worn out that he fell to the floor and went to sleep on his way to bed.

He held on until October 1890, when winter began to signal its unwelcome return. In the face of this appalling prospect even the man who could never bring himself to admit failure, admitted failure. He was, as he told a friend, "busted." He had lost more than $3 million. And so the great quarry was abandoned. The sale of the remnants of the equipment brought in just enough money to pay off the residue of debt—and brought on a lawsuit against Edison from some other investors who felt that they should have been kept more fully informed.

Perhaps they should have, for Edison had not been idle during his irregular absences from the quarry. He was already deeply involved in the development of motion pictures.

# Sigmund Freud
# and the
# "Dream Book"

S igmund Freud's father had told him that he would never amount to anything, and at the turn of the century the world seemed to agree. Although the last half-dozen years of the nineteenth century may have been the most productive of Freud's life, that period ended not with a bang or even a whimper, but rather in a stony silence punctuated by occasional vilification.

It was a productive period but also a laborious and difficult one. Freud was spending about ten hours a day with his patients and filling his off hours with what a follower has called "intensive mental activity such as is rarely permitted to anyone." During this time he developed psychoanalysis as a therapeutic technique, as well as his theories of repression and resistance. He examined how the former can affect memory, linking it with common lapses of forgetfulness. He introduced the role of sexual experience into the study of neuroses, including the influence of infant sexuality. And he brought to the world of psychology the revolutionary, but ultimately irrepressible, notion of the Oedipus complex.

That notion appeared for the first time in *The Interpretation of*

111

*Dreams.* Eventually this book would be considered his greatest work, containing his most perceptive writing, offering his most significant contribution. It represented work so thorough, so painstaking, that it has been changed very little in the many editions that have followed its initial publication. It also represented some thirty months of concentrated, meticulous writing under a burden of chronic insecurity and intermittent anxiety. For Freud was a man of mercurial moods, ranging from unraveling despair with his work on one day to buoyant optimism over it on the next. It was only many years later that he was able to say of the book, "Insight like this comes only once in a lifetime."

He had special reason to feel insecure these days, for this was a time of professional isolation. He was a Jew in Vienna and a maverick in a milieu tightly controlled by a very conservative establishment. In meetings of the Vienna Neurological Society his views on the sexual aspects of neurosis met with icy stares and cold shoulders. His quarantine had its advantages, of course, since his work was never impeded by a burden of unavoidable social commitments.

He had been interested in dreams for a long time. So had many others—seers, sorcerers, fortune-tellers, witch doctors, mystics—but not as a subject of scientific study undertaken to determine their causes and significance. Indeed, psychology as a science had given up attempts to make any sense out of dreams, attributing them casually to uninhibited imagination stimulated by immediate sensations or recent memories, or simply arising by pure chance. The idea of writing a book on the subject apparently occurred to Freud as early as 1886, with subsequent years devoted to such organizing of his data and his thought as circumstances would permit. He wrote much later that the book was essentially finished early in 1896, although the writing of it was not completed until mid-1899 and it was not formally published until early 1900. He began the writing, it seems, partly for a very personal reason. He was suffering from a bout of low spirits and felt that the effort at self-expression would prove good therapy. His thoroughgoing research into the existing scientific literature on dreams also prompted the maverick in him to get on with the project, since the general consensus (notably excepting the second-century Greek Artemidorus) was that dreams are inexplicable nonsense.

This he refused to believe on the basis of his own experience with hundreds of patients. Dreams—not merely their "manifest" content, which will be remembered on waking, but also their "latent" content buried in the unconscious—are the result, he wrote, of five particular mechanisms. Through *condensation*, the manifest part of a dream may only briefly summarize the latent element, which can entail several levels of meaning. Through *displacement*, the dreamer's mind eludes its censor by substitution, as when a little girl dreams of breaking her doll's head instead of her brother's. In *representation*, the mind uses concrete images to stand for abstract concepts and relationships, as when someone who feels restricted dreams of being in prison, evidently because the dreaming mind cannot handle abstractions. Related to displacement is *symbolization*, which permits the dreamer to get by the censor by substituting symbols for erotic images—swords and umbrellas (etc., etc.) for the male organ, for example, and ovens and rooms with doors (etc., etc.) for the female. Finally there is the mechanism of *secondary elaboration*, which occurs after waking up and during the effort to reconstruct the dream, a process (especially in analysis) that can reveal even more than the dream itself. Behind these mechanisms, providing the psychic energy, lies the desire for wish fulfillment, for making something come true which in reality is impracticable or forbidden.

The book ricochets between brilliant insights and precarious non sequiturs, and Freud himself revealed in his letters a large measure of ambivalence toward it. On one occasion he wrote despairingly that it all added up to a bloated truism—dreamers universally want to sleep and therefore have dreams to keep from waking up. On another occasion he decided that the book represented his "finest discovery, the only one likely to outlive me." In the end, as the manuscript went off to the printers late in

1899, he felt on the whole fairly happy about it.

But readers and reviewers did not share his euphoria. Of the 600 copies in the first printing, only 123 were sold in the first six weeks, 351 in the first two years, and the full 600 only after eight years. A year and a half after its publication Freud lamented in a letter that he had yet to discover a single notice in any medical or other scientific journal. A newspaper in Vienna ran a nasty review of the book six weeks after publication, and sales in that important city dried up altogether. Over the next six or seven months reviews also appeared in two Berlin papers, not so nasty but not very enthusiastic either. Ironically, a professor at Vienna's Psychiatric Clinic was widely reported as commenting, in a lecture on hysteria, "These ill people wish to relieve their minds, and a colleague in this city has taken advantage of this need to make up a theory about it in order to fill his pockets."

Despite the professional indifference toward the book, often lapsing into derision, Freud remained a popular lecturer. But an illustrative incident occurred one day when a student who had attended several lectures asked if he might walk home with Freud and talk about *The Interpretation of Dreams*. During their stroll he explained that he had written a thesis against Freud's theories. In preparing it he had asked his professors whether he should read the "dream book" but had been told that it really wasn't worth the effort. Now, having been impressed by the lectures, he alleged, he greatly regretted following their advice. He regretted his thesis even more, but it was too late to recall it from publication. He assured Freud, however, that he now considered the doctor's theories to be as solid as Roman Catholic doctrines—a remark that may have revealed something about his beliefs and motivation, and that surely must have left Freud reeling.

Ten years later the publisher brought out a second edition of *The Interpretation of Dreams*. Six more editions were published in Freud's lifetime. The book was eventually translated into many languages, including English, Russian, Spanish, French, Swedish,

Hungarian, Czech, and Japanese. Toward the end of 1900 Freud wrote a condensed version, which received still wider distribution. In later years the critical student, having become a frequent book critic for a medical journal, regularly made fun of it.

# The Wright Brothers and Sales Resistance

In January 1905 the U.S. Army's Board of Ordnance and Fortification received a letter from Wilbur and Orville Wright of Dayton, Ohio:

Sirs:

The series of aeronautical experiments upon which we have been engaged for the past five years has ended in the production of a flying machine of a type fitted for practical use. It not only flies through the air at high speed, but it also lands without being wrecked. During the year 1904 one hundred and five flights were made at our experimenting station, on the Huffman prairie, east of the city; and though our experience in handling the machine has been too short to give any high degree of skill, we nevertheless succeeded, toward the end of the season, in making two flights of five minutes each, in which we sailed round and round the field until a distance of about three miles had been covered, at a speed of thirty-five miles an hour....

The numerous flights in straight lines, in circles, and over S-shaped courses, in calms and in winds, have made it quite certain that flying has been brought to a point where it can be made of great practical use in various ways, one of which is that of scouting and carrying messages in time of war. If the latter features are of interest to our own government, we shall be pleased to take the matter up either on a basis of providing machines of agreed specification, at a contract price, or of furnishing all the scientific and practical information we have accumulated in these years of experimenting, together with a license to use our patents; thus putting the government in a position to operate on its own account.

If you can find it convenient to ascertain whether this is a subject of interest to our own government, it would oblige us greatly, as early information on this point will aid us in making our plans for the future.

This letter was not very different from the several dozen on the same subject that were now arriving in the board's mail each year. Nor was its reply unusual—it could not underwrite experiments, but would seriously consider contracting for a flying machine capable of "practical operation." The reply may well have been essentially a form letter; the writer (it was signed by a General Gillespie of the Army General Staff) seems not to have read the Wrights' letter very meticulously. In any case, its lack of enthusiasm so irritated the Wrights that they interpreted it as an unqualified rejection. What they had forgotten was their—especially Wilbur's—obsession with secrecy, and its effect on others.

The more easygoing Orville, now thirty-three, tended to follow the lead of his more vigorous brother Wilbur, now thirty-seven, and they worked together very smoothly. As a result, they had somehow managed to conduct those 105 test flights without the slightest public notice, despite widespread curiosity about powered flight. They were far ahead of any competition—so they strongly believed, and later events proved them right—chiefly because their careful observations of soaring birds, translated into mathematical calculations, had resulted in a "triaxial" flyer that could not only turn left and right and nose up and down but also rotate on its longitudinal axis, the axis along its flight direction. This last capability, achieved through an ingenious warping or twisting of the wings one way and another during flight, permitted banking on turns and thereby enormously improved maneuverability. It was a unique feature of the Wrights' flying machine, one that made the difference between a soaring and a wallowing kind of flight.

If they had made this clear in their letter, the army board might have been more attentive. But this feature was precisely the sort of thing that made the brothers so secretive. Not only was it ingenious, it also was simple and therefore could be easily copied. Their five years of laborious and painstaking experiments had resulted in a machine that invited imitation by anyone with the requisite greed and cunning. And so they were determined to protect themselves with some sort of ironclad contract before divulging any information on how their machine operated. Notable is the absence, in the letter, of any invitation for an army representative to observe their machine in flight.

Indeed, Wilbur's acceptance of the army's reply as a rejection may have been due partly to a fear that the government, if it genuinely recognized the machine's unique capabilities and potential, might simply appropriate the whole project—the machine, the design, the test results, everything—to prevent any sale to a foreign government. So it may have been with some relief that the brothers now felt free to turn to England. They did so, offering to sell their flyer for $2,500, that amount to be paid for each machine demonstrated in a test flight after the contract was signed. (They hoped the test flights would cover between fifty and one hundred miles.) The British were mildly interested. In May they wrote that they would ask their military attaché in Washington to arrange for a demonstration flight. Apparently the Wrights had failed to make it clear that the demonstrations would have to come *after* the signing of the contract. This confusion proved irrelevant, however, because the attaché never did get in touch with them.

In June the Wrights resumed their flight testing, pushing the machine into ever longer and higher flights—long enough (twenty miles in thirty-three minutes) and high enough (sixty feet) to attract the notice of passengers on a nearby interurban trolley. As the summer wore on the brothers came to realize that the secrecy surrounding their work could not be maintained much longer and that potential buyers were likely to demand some reliable evidence or testimony concerning the flyer's hardly credible performance. During the summer testing, therefore, they took photographs of the machine in flight, at various impressive angles, and in October arranged a demonstration flight for a gathering of fifteen respectable Daytonians pledged to secrecy until the brothers gave the word. Wilbur did the flying that day, rising to sixty feet and staying aloft for thirty-eight minutes and for a distance of twenty-four miles. But his performance briefly blew their cover, for some trolley riders reported seeing the flyer and the witnesses out at Huffman's field, the newspapers extracted the story from one of the secrecy-bound witnesses, and the next day a crowd gathered at the field—only to learn that the Wrights had dismantled their machine and had stolen away as silently as the proverbial Arabs. They would not fly again until May 1908, over 30 months later.

A few days after their strategic retreat the brothers, having heard nothing further from the British, sent a letter to Secretary of War William Howard Taft, who bucked it to, of course, the Board of Ordinance and Fortification. This second letter was characteristically cryptic, offering neither information on the recent test flights nor any explanation of how scores of flights could have been kept so tightly secret for such a long time. It made no mention of photographs or eyewitnesses. It simply proposed a contract like the one to which the British had reacted with such guarded circumspection. A machine would be supplied for trials after a contract had been signed, with purchase contingent upon performance. The board replied about a week later that it could not underwrite experiments but would be happy to have more information on the design and construction of the flyer in order to assess its practicality. No, the Wrights countered in their distrustful answer, *you* tell *us* what you require of such a machine and we will assess the practicality of the requirements. The board, having not the dimmest notion of the potentiality of an aeroplane, was hardly in a position to draw up specifications. Its response, therefore, was a rather testy put-up-or-shut-up letter. The Wrights, instead of taking a course in business correspondence, simply nursed their resentment in silence.

This silence applied only to the U.S. Army, but an exchange with the British proved no more fruitful. The attaché, the British insisted, was available to observe a test flight but was not empowered to enter into any contracts. The Wrights replied that, if he came to Dayton, he could interview a large number of eyewitnesses, but the British countered that eyewitness accounts of powered flights were a penny a dozen—and thereupon terminated the negotiations, such as they were.

Next it was the turn of the French, who reacted to the Wrights' approach much more immediately and positively. The War Ministry dispatched an agent to negotiate a contract, and by early January it was signed: one practical, reproducible flying machine for a million francs. Of this amount, a fortieth was paid in cash at once, without conditions, and the rest was put in two months' escrow. The French government was to have exclusive rights to the machine and all design details for the next three months (excepting only the U.S. government, in the unlikely event that it should become interested). Everything seemed pretty well wrapped up.

And then it all came apart. The French military began picking at the contract in a display of sober second thoughts, inspired possibly by a vague expectation that French inventors were hovering on the verge of an aeronautical breakthrough. A delegation of French officers clandestinely visited Dayton with several demands, chiefly for a year of exclusive rights and for a capability of flying at an altitude of 1,000 feet. The Wrights resisted. Even the help of the respected, Paris-born aerodynamicist Octave Chanute was not enough to break the impasse, and the deal fell through. The Wrights, despite the forfeited down payment, were wearily disheartened.

In some desperation they decided that promotion might require some publicity and that secrecy might not be the best form of publicity. Releasing the witnesses of the October 1905 flight from their pledge of secrecy, they sent a list of the names to *The Scientific American*, which soon published a very persuasive account of its interviews with the witnesses. Senator Henry Cabot Lodge of Massachusetts, on the strength of this article, recommended that the Board of Ordnance and Fortification have an agent visit Dayton to see the flying machine in operation. The board wrote the brothers, who replied that they would offer proof but not flight demonstrations. This exchange, like the others, died in futility.

But in November an event near Paris brought the brothers up short. A young Brazilian named Alberto Santos-Dumont, who had a reputation for sensational experiments with dirigibles, flew a powered machine a distance of more than 700 feet. Although the accounts of the awkward flight gave the Wrights no great concern, they were disturbed by the growing popular belief that mankind was about to take off into a full-blown air age. The more widely that belief was enhanced by their rivals, the less attention was likely to be paid to *them*.

Casting about for a new approach, they applied to Charles R. Flint, an affluent risk-taker who had been involved in the early development of the submarine and the automobile and who had very impressive connections both domestically and abroad. With his support and advice over the next thirty months or so, they muddled through several more disappointments, crowned by a tedious visit to Europe in the summer and fall of 1907. Not only were their days there filled with time-consuming, demeaning suppliance in the waiting rooms of French, English, and German bureaucracies, but such publicity as they received was generally humiliating ("bluffers" was a popular comment). And it was all for nothing. No one knew how far ahead of their rivals the Wrights were technically, and the brothers were afraid to tell them without the protection of a contract. One opportunity afforded them entailed a bribe, when a public servant offered to arrange a satisfactory contract for a side payment of $50,000. Wilbur frostily agreed to this arrangement with the stipulation that the official's assistance and price be particularized in the contract. The arrangement died stillborn.

On their return to America, however, the Wrights found that the U.S. Army, alarmed by the apparent successes of their rivals in Europe, had developed a renewed interest in whatever they had to offer. In February 1908 the board signed a contingency contract, with official trials set for the following September. And in March, through Flint's determined efforts, a French commercial syndicate signed on with a similarly satisfying contract. By May the brothers were flying once again, at Kitty Hawk and at Kill Devil Hills in North Carolina, now less concerned with concealing their achievements. The newspaper reporters made the most of their new lease on life.

The French trials came first, in August. They demonstrated just how advanced the Wrights' machine was when Wilbur's first banking maneuver made the fascinated spectators gasp and cry out in alarm. This was not the level, stiff, and awkward flight that they had seen their compatriots achieve. It displayed, rather, the controlled grace of a soaring bird. After Wilbur had brought his machine in to a graceful landing, he was mobbed. No more derision. Only unstinting adulation. A French aviator in the crowd was later described as shaking his head in near-disbelief. "In comparison with the Wrights," he was quoted as saying, "we are like children."

Meanwhile, back in America, Orville was preparing for the U.S. Army tests, which began early in September. They also were spectacularly successful, including a flight of seventy-four minutes at 200 feet. The series of trials on both sides of the Atlantic continued in this vein for several weeks, interrupted only by a tragedy on this side, when a hairline crack in a propeller caused a crash and the death of a young army lieutenant riding along as an observer. But there was no longer any doubt, anywhere, of the Wrights' preeminence in the science, and art, of human flight.

# Pablo Picasso and *Les Demoiselles d'Avignon*

One day in the late spring or early summer of 1907, Pablo Picasso was wandering through the Museum of Comparative Sculpture in Paris. Coming upon an unfamiliar door, he opened it and found himself in an exhibition of African sculpture. Even years late, a friend has reported, he spoke very emotionally about the intensity of his reaction to that display of primitive art. Years later also, in an interview, he flatly denied having seen any African art at this time, but then his attitude toward truth, as well as toward art, was often that of the unregenerate pixie that inhabited him all his life.

In 1907 he was still one of a teeming myriad of impoverished artists for whom Paris was again the scene of a revolution, although a revolution much different from that of 1789. Partly because of the introduction, and threat, of photography, the artistic community was in a ferment of radical innovation. Picasso himself was already in the process of fundamental change.

Until now his work had been relatively representational, even conventional, by standards of the past. In his Blue Period he had depicted the loneliness of old age, poverty, and infirmity in plainly human terms. In his Rose Period he had shown a happier, more carefree life in his picture of harlequins and clowns and other circus people, all easily recognizable. But now he had been laboring for several months over a large canvas showing a number of very peculiar-looking nudes posing nonchalantly before the viewer. As he developed the picture, as he modified it through successive drawings and watercolor sketches, the women grew ever more abstract and geometrical, becoming sharp-angled versions of Paul Cézanne's famous bathers. And two of their faces took on the aspect of grotesque African masks.

If these distortions were partly a reaction to the lasciviously luscious female nudes of half a century earlier, it was a very severe reaction indeed, perhaps reflecting some of the severity in Picasso's Spanish heritage. His own title for the picture was "Avignon Whorehouse," and he was deeply irritated when it came to be called "The Damsels of Avignon" in a pious rechristening that amounted to evisceration. The painting, representing as it did a bold, abrupt, even defiant departure from the generally prevailing criteria of artistic practice, must have given even a dedicated maverick like Picasso some nervous moments. How would it be received? What would it be in the eye of the beholder?

When the work was finished, or as nearly finished as it was ever likely to be, Picasso began showing it to beholders in whose eyes he expected to see sympathetic appreciation, his friends and fellow artists. The exotic poet Guillaume Apollinaire, who had urged the need for shock in any effort to break away from dead tradition, evidently disliked the shock he felt at his first sight of the painting. After recovering, he offered a vague, shopworn, and rather cowardly comment to the effect that it was certainly revolutionary, complained about its lack of sentiment, and confessed that he simply didn't understand it. If such comments had come from a stuffy academician, Picasso could have dismissed them easily with a disdainful shrug. But Apollinaire welcomed innovation and was to be in the vanguard of the critics supporting abstract art and particularly the introduction of cubism—of which, ironically, *Les Demoiselles d'Avignon* is today considered the outstanding, as well as priceless, harbinger.

Picasso's experience with the Steins—the famous Gertrude and her brother Leo—was at least as dispiriting. They thought it unworthy of his talent and certainly unworthy of their critical appreciation. He had, they complained, betrayed the great confidence that they had shown in his earlier work. If he continued on this path, he would find it "finished." From that time on, Picasso was soon less and less at the Steins' Saturday soirees, and Gertrude in her later books about him deftly skirted any mention of the painting. The rift undoubtedly was widened when Picasso, at a party, happened to overhear a conversation between Henri Matisse and Leo in which he was subjected to a succession of unflattering remarks. Matisse, doubtless influenced by his rivalry with Picasso and a wish to ingratiate himself with the Steins, declared that Picasso was making fun of modern trends in art and that he, Matisse, would see that his satirical colleague would be amply repaid for such ridicule. Thereafter the friendly rivalry between the two men hardened into enduring hostility.

Even Georges Braque, Picasso's partner in abstraction, reacted to the picture violently and, in rather elementary terms, accused Picasso of losing control. Such extreme distortions of human figures must arise out of a passionate disregard for technique, for precision, for craftsmanship. These figures were monstrosities—look at those noses! More than merely negative in his criticism, Braque was so profoundly distressed that he returned to his own studio and remained voluntarily incommunicado for several days.

A professional critic from *La Revue Blanche* reacted much less violently but no less negatively. His weapon was the stiletto of condescension. The work was "interesting," he told Picasso, recommending that he develop his talent for caricature. But the unkindest cut was probably André Derain's description of the painting as "a desperate project. Some day they'll discover Picasso hanged behind it." Even among the shopkeepers in the neighborhood rumors were spreading that Picasso had lost his mind.

An affluent young German named Daniel-Henry Kahnweiler had recently arrived in Paris and opened a picture gallery. Partial to Cézanne and Gauguin, he also bought and exhibited some Fauve paintings, including those of Braque and Derain. He knew nothing of Picasso's work until a friend mentioned the outlandish painting by an artist whose signature Kahnweiler thought he vaguely remembered seeing on some drawings at an obscure gallery. His curiosity sharply whetted, he paid Picasso a visit in the latter's studio. His first and apparently greatest shock was caused by the sight of Picasso's poverty. He later described the artist as "incredibly heroic" to live in such destitution. As for the painting, which his friend had described as "Assyrian," he was deeply moved by it and judged it to be at least an important piece of work. He offered to buy it and anything else that Picasso had ready for sale. The painter, still smarting from the reactions to his masterwork, informed his new patron that the painting was still incomplete and was not for sale. He did, however, sell Kahnweiler several other things, including the sketches and drawings that had led up to the painting. Some time after Kahnweiler left, Picasso rolled up *Les Demoiselles* and relegated it to a pile in the corner of the studio. It would not be seen again for eighteen years.

In the summer of 1925 a friend persuaded him to exhume the painting and mount it because an important collector, Jacques Doucet, had expressed an interest in it. When Doucet arrived, his reaction to Picasso's studio was clearly the same as Kahnweiler's, but so was his reaction to the painting. Assured that it was for sale, he offered Picasso an incredible 25,000 francs for it. The painter accepted the offer with flabbergasted alacrity.

Forty years later the painting would bring 350,000 francs, or about $70,000. Since then its price has similarly risen to more than a million dollars.

# Eugene O'Neill and the Bottle

"None of us can help the things life has done to us. They're done before you realize it, and once they're done they make you do other things until at last everything comes between you and what you'd like to be, and you've lost your true self forever."

This cry of despair comes from Mary Tyrone in Eugene O'Neill's *Long Day's Journey Into Night*. As that largely autobiographical play revealed, O'Neill was born into a quite unusual family troubled by a curse that was very much as Mary Tyrone (the dramatic counterpart of his mother) described it. The thing that life had done to his mother was morphine addiction, brought on by a doctor's prescription to relieve pain after surgery. Life had trapped his thespian father, James, into a lucrative but frustrating and even humiliating career: Although longing to do "serious" roles, he played Edmund Dantes in more than 5,000 productions of *The Count of Monte Cristo*, only to be known in the end (as his son predicted to him) as the father of Eugene O'Neill. Both of his sons inherited his devotion to whiskey, which aggravated their spirit of rebellion against his tendency to dominate. The elder, James, Jr., had to leave Notre Dame University , for example, after a drinking spree in which he appeared at one of the college's formal dances with a notorious neighborhood tart on his arm; he died at forty-five in a sanatorium, an alcoholic to the bitter end. Eugene largely followed suit, missing only the bitter end, by a hair.

Katharine Hepburn reportedly once said of the Irish, in reference to her friend Spencer Tracy, "They cry a lot, you know." Like his father and brother, O'Neill found relief from this burden of tears in the bottle. He also found relief from inhibitions, and in classic style while at Princeton he engaged in extracurricular activities that got a nice girl, Kathleen Jenkins, "in trouble." His father, influenced by memories of his own early escapades, urged his son not to marry the girl, since marriage could entail a long-standing commitment for which Eugene obviously was unsuited. The son took this advice with discrimination, marrying the girl in 1909 and then deserting her until their divorce some three years later.

The desertion intensified his affair with the bottle. Soon after the pathetic wedding he sailed for Honduras on a "prospecting" trip underwritten by his father. It produced no gold, but it did give him plenty of latent material for *The Emperor Jones*. After only a few months he came down with jungle fever and returned to New York, where he spent a little time with his father's theatrical company. Despite frequent attacks of remorse, dulled by frequent recourse to analgesic liquor, he avoided any contact with his wife and child. Early in 1910 he rebelled, mildly, against his father's wishes and took a job on a sailing ship bound for Buenos Aires. The trip there took two months and gave him an addiction to the sea almost as irresistible as his addiction to alcohol, at least emotionally. It was the latter addiction, however, that he cultivated intensively for about a year in Buenos Aires, where, he remarked later, probably every park bench at one time or another "served him as a bed." This period of carefree misery and destitution was interrupted only by a brief job with some American firms in the city and by a quick trip as a seaman on a cattle boat to South Africa and back.

This lifestyle continued after he returned to New York in the spring of 1911. Kathleen wanted a divorce and, since adultery constituted the only legal grounds in that state, he arranged to be "surprised" in bed with a prostitute. For three dollars a month he rented a room above Jimmy-the-Priest's saloon, not surprisingly spending more time in the saloon than in the room, drinking purposefully and unremittingly with other habitués of like calling, very much in the manner of *The Iceman Cometh*. As for the proprietor, who was given his name because of his ascetic look, O'Neill described "Johnny-the-Priest" in *Anna Christie:* "With his pale, thin, clean-shaven face, mild blue eyes and white hair, a cassock would seem more suited to him than the apron he wears. Neither his voice nor his general manner dispels this illusion, which has made him a personage on the waterfront. They are soft and bland. But beneath all his mildness one senses the man behind the mask—cynical, callous, hard as nails." Jimmy would permit mugging at his bar, but no fighting.

O'Neill's room was cold and grimy, its darkness relieved by a single small kerosene lamp, its space taken up mostly by two cots. Besides the several varieties of bugs, O'Neill had to share this luxury with whoever happened to have three dollars that month. He lived on cheap whiskey and the free bowl of soup served to roomers each day at lunchtime. He spent his time sleeping (or "sleeping it off"), chatting and singing with barmates, strolling aimlessly along the waterfront, and loafing luxuriously in Battery Park, which occupied a place in his heart second only to Jimmy's bar. And whoring. When his slim funds supporting all these amenities ran out in July, he joined a red-haired Irish giant named Driscoll on a trip to England. Driscoll was a stoker, O'Neill was an ordinary seaman, and the ship was the S.S. *New York*, a luxury passenger liner. O'Neill's pay was fifty-five dollars for the round trip.

He had fallen in love with the sea on the sailing ship, but his work on the liner was "ugly, tedious." And humiliating, since he was very sensitive to being patronized by hoity-toity passengers. Driscoll's job as a stoker was worse, if better-paying, so bad that sometimes a stoker would thrust his head into the coal chute so that he would be knocked unconscious by the falling coal and get a little rest. These men, among the largest and strongest in the crew, black with smoke and coal dust, looked like menacing simian monsters to anyone unfamiliar with the sight. In *The Hairy Ape,* the reaction of Mildred, the bored socialite, to the sight of Yank the stoker is to cry out, "Oh, the filthy beast!" before falling in a maidenly swoon. But O'Neill liked Driscoll, admiring his individualism, his strength of character, his irrepressibility.

When O'Neill returned to New York he collected his pay, reduced by forty dollars for expenditures in the ship's canteen, and settled back in at Jimmy's, which he described, essentially, in *The Iceman Cometh* as the "No Chance Saloon. It's Bedrock Bar, the End of the Line Café, the Bottom of the Sea Rathskeller...the last harbor. No one here has to worry about where they're going next, because there is no farther they can go." In this end-of-the-line atmosphere he was shocked one day to hear that Driscoll, the indomitable Driscoll, had committed suicide, throwing himself into the sea from a passenger liner.

What this news did for O'Neill's own death wish can well be imagined. That he had a death wish, or at least a preoccupation with death, seems likely from his life and his plays. As his biographers Arthur and Barbara Gelb have pointed out, in twenty-five of his forty-five published plays, forty of the characters "suffer violent or unnatural deaths. Of these, nine are suicides. Twenty-one of the poisoned, diseased, mangled, strangled, sliced, drowned, electrocuted, cremated or bullet-ridden men, women and children meet their ends in full view of the audience." And in *Lazarus Laughed,* "There are twenty-seven references to death in Act I alone."

Death wish or no, O'Neill did attempt suicide in the fall of 1911. Such attempts are often deliberate failures, but this one seems to have been the genuine article, even though it had its comic aspect. He collected Veronal tablets, which at the time could be bought in small quantities without a prescription, in several visits to drugstores in the vicinity. When he had what he considered enough for the purpose, he climbed to his room at Jimmy's and gulped down the lot. There he was found comatose by a couple of well-oiled friends just returned from a high old time in the saloon below. The empty Veronal bottles lying about suggested what he had done, and fortunately the two tosspots were alert enough to take action. Much pacing back and forth and prodigious drafts of coffee brought him around after a while. By the time they got him to Bellevue Hospital for a checkup, he had recovered almost completely. As a result, he was certified to be in good health and allowed to go home. But his friends were held and assigned to the alcoholic ward.

His health may have been passable in a casual physical examination, but it was seriously undermined by the kind of life that he had been leading. Even after his father took him home to New London in 1912 for several months rest (at least such rest as that suggested in *Long Day's Journey*), he grew ill and had to be taken to a tuberculosis sanatarium at the end of the year. And there he began writing his first plays.

Seven years later his first major New York play, *Beyond the Horizon,* won him the Pulitzer prize. And forty years later, in December 1953, shortly after his death, Brooks Atkinson wrote in the *New York Times,* "A giant writer has dropped off the earth; a great spirit and our greatest dramatist has left us, and our theater world is now a smaller, more ordinary place."

Except that it still has his plays.

# Winston Churchill and Gallipoli

$\mathbf{B}$y the early days of 1915 the great war had become stalled along a blood-soaked line of trenches strung out across the face of Europe. A growing number of people in the British government were becoming convinced that the only way to break the stalemate would be some sort of end run, probably around the southern flank. In their vanguard was the First Lord of the Admiralty Winston Churchill. "Are there not other alternatives," he had asked in December 1914, "than sending our armies to chew barbed wire in Flanders?"

Doubtless he was influenced by the lack of opportunities for the Admiralty in trench warfare. Action was what he lived for, although it could get him into trouble. During the previous October he had seen plenty of action in Antwerp, not as top sea dog but as an emissary of his immediate superior, Horatio Kitchener, the war minister. The Belgian army and some 8000 British troops were desperately trying to hold Antwerp against the German juggernaut, and Lord Kitchener could think of no one better qualified than the bulldog Churchill to stiffen their resolve. Although Churchill joined the battle just in time to participate in the inevitable retreat, he did stiffen Allied resistance enough for an important delaying action. Because of that resistance and delay, the bulk of the troops had time to flood the lowlands and escape, thereby denying the Germans an opportunity to use the Channel ports for launching an assault on England. Nevertheless, since this value of the delay went generally unrecognized, Churchill was blamed for a disastrous defeat and became the butt of stinging criticism and ribald rebukes.

Thus he was hardly in a position, only a couple of months later, to push for a new, bold, and rather unconventional military strategy. But Russia's Grand Duke Nicholas unintentionally gave him an opening. In a wire early in January 1915, the Grand Duke implored Kitchener and Prime Minister Herbert Asquith to create a diversion, a military feint, that would force Turkey to pull back some troops from the Caucasus. And so Kitchener and Asquith, agreeing that Russia badly needed help, began to think of Churchill's southern end run. And of Gallipoli.

That narrow peninsula, jutting into the Mediterranean (or Aegean) Sea at Turkey's northwest corner, was inviting—so inviting that the plans to attack it were continued after the Grand Duke withdrew his plea because of an unexpected Turkish defeat near the Russian border. The peninsula formed the northern shore of the Dardanelles. These straits led northeastward into the small Sea of Marmara, to Constantinople, and thence into the Black Sea and its many Russian ports. Control of the straits could give the Allies a secure supply route to Russia, cut Turkey off from the Central Powers, expose Austria-Hungary to direct attack along a Balkan front, drain enemy strength from the western front, and shorten the war by months, perhaps many months. In Berlin the naval war minister, Admiral Alfred von Tirpitz, was arguing (unbeknownst to London, of course) that the loss of the Dardanelles would mean the loss of the war. It was all enough to make Churchill's mouth water.

But Kitchener's mouth did not water so easily. He proved stubbornly reluctant to commit any land forces to the enterprise. Churchill's immediate subordinate, First Sea Lord Sir John

Fisher, insisted almost as stubbornly that naval forces alone could not do the job. Churchill, who at forty-one had a long-standing love-hate relationship with the seventy-four-year-old Fisher, over- rode his objections and, supported by the entire War Council, ordered the naval commander in the area, a vice admiral named Carden, to begin the assault.

Carden did so on February 19 and was immediately stymied by almost a week of foul weather. He renewed the attack on the twenty-fifth, bombarding the forts on both shores of the channel with his force of nearly two dozen major ships. The Turkish guns near the entrance to the straits were silenced, and soon British sailors had landed to blow up the forts while the Turks hastily retreated. Things looked very promising. Carden was elated. So was Churchill.

However, as British minesweepers ventured farther into the channel, approaching the narrows where Leander and Lord Byron had done their famous swimming exercises, the remaining Turkish forts turned them back with a heavy barrage. As the sweepers retreated, Turkish infantry troops drove the British landing parties back to their ships. And Admiral Carden suffered a nervous breakdown. But not Churchill.

The latter's disappointment over the setback was greatly light- ened early in March by a telegram from Greece pledging three divisions and naval support for another try at Gallipoli. It gave impetus to the planning for a return engagement. It also was typical of the Gallipoli campaign, for within about twenty-four hours the idea of any Greek help was entirely canceled by a telegram from the Czar, who in a burst of near-suicidal greed flatly refused to cooperate in any action that might permit Greeks to reach Constantinople before the Russians.

Nevertheless Carden's replacement, Vice Admiral John de Roebeck, launched an all-out assault on the morning of March 18. By 2:00 that afternoon the Turks were very nearly defeated. Many of their guns had been destroyed, their communications were in a shambles, and they were almost out of ammunition. Had the

British known how close the Turks were to capitulation, they could almost certainly have finished the job. But they did not know it, and at this precise moment events took a nasty turn. The straits were laced with mines, and the Turks had been very coy about revealing their locations. With dismaying suddenness six capital ships of the fleet, struck by mines, were sunk or otherwise put out of action. De Roebeck, shocked by the losses, ordered a withdrawal and advised London that the straits could not be taken by naval action alone. He did this over the protests of a staff officer who insisted that the Turks were virtually beaten and could not defend the straits against another naval attack. Back in London, Churchill's similar protests were similarly overruled. After the war it was discovered that the Turks also thought they were beaten, as indeed they were. They were quite astonished by the Allied withdrawal. Their commander later reported that another attack would have totally defeated them and knocked Turkey out of the war.

Kitchener was now trapped by his own feeling that the Allies must not suffer the humiliation of a defeat by such a mere appendage as Turkey; no further pressure from Churchill was necessary. A force of about five divisions, including some French and Australians, was hastily put together and shipped to the area, arriving in mid-April. Meanwhile, however, the Turks, pressed by the now alarmed Germans, had assembled a defending force of some six divisions and were lying in wait. As a result, when the Allied troops attacked the peninsula on April 25, they were repulsed. Bloodily.

The next week or so was a period of attack and counterattack amid garbled communications and general confusion on both sides. With the conflict apparently settling into a stalemate as frustrating as that on the western front, the naval commanders in the area decided that another naval assault on the Dardanelles might do the trick. Admiral de Roebeck then promptly informed London of this consensus.

His telegram promoted a meeting between Churchill and

Fisher on May 11. Churchill essentially agreed with the proposal, but Fisher crustily refused to authorize any naval action until the Turks were defeated on land. Although Churchill might have won this argument eventually, on the next day news that an old but serviceable battleship had been sunk in the Dardanelles so alarmed Fisher that he determined to order the newest and most powerful ship of the fleet, the *Queen Elizabeth*, to leave the area at once. This decision enraged Kitchener, and Churchill apparently had all he could do to keep the two men from personal combat.

Their hostility enlivened the next meeting of the War Council on May 14, with Kitchener complaining of betrayal and Fisher asserting that he had opposed the whole Gallipoli adventure from the beginning. Churchill tried to steer the meeting into a discussion of the current predicament, proposing that the Allies at Gallipoli be supported with enough reinforcements and naval firepower to take the peninsula. Without any backing from the fuming Fisher, however, he could not be very persuasive, and the meeting adjourned without reaching a decision. Yet that night Churchill managed to reach an agreement with Fisher on reinforcements for de Roebeck. After Fisher had gone to bed, Churchill added a couple of submarines to the list as an afterthought and then sent the list to Fisher's office for his concurrence first thing in the morning.

To his consternation, that afterthought was just the thing to light Fisher's very short fuse. Before the morning was out Churchill received a formal letter of resignation from his First Sea Lord, who, the letter informed him, had already left for Scotland. Even though Fisher was found before he left London and was persuaded to come back for a meeting at No. 10 Downing Street, he spurned the efforts of both Asquith and Churchill toward a reconciliation. He would resume the office only if Asquith would give him complete control of the navy and would fire Churchill. Instead, Asquith frostily accepted his resignation.

That resignation proved to be Churchill's undoing. His Majesty's Loyal Opposition seized the opportunity, informing Asquith that they intended to challenge his administration's conduct of the war, perhaps to the point of demanding a vote of confidence in the House of Commons. Asquith, capitulating, asked for negotiations toward forming a coalition government. The opposition demanded Churchill's head. Churchill tried to mollify them, but they were adamant.

His last day at the Admiralty was May 26. Although the Gallipoli campaign was to drag on, intermittently, for another seven months, it was already widely recognized as a disaster. The opposition press blamed Churchill almost exclusively, and most of his colleagues who had approved the campaign developed convenient lapses of memory for the occasion. He was generally identified as the author of the navy's losses, the army's setbacks, the failures in communication, the shortages of ammunition, the inadequacy of command, and the thousands of casualties—which were to reach a quarter of a million on the Allied side by the end of the campaign, including the death of the poet Rupert Brooke. Whatever had gone wrong, it was Churchill's fault. The condemnation was universal—almost. Churchill's removal, wrote Lloyd George, was "a cruel and unjust degradation. The Dardanelles failure was due not so much to Mr. Churchill's precipitancy as to Lord Kitchener's and Mr. Asquith's procrastination."

This was perfectly true, a fact that made the din of recrimination all the harder to bear, even for the resilient Churchill. Violet Bonham Carter, Asquith's daughter and Churchill's close friend, later wrote of the tears in his eyes, as well as in her own, as he told her despairingly. "I'm finished—I'm done." A newspaper correspondent who had not seen him for a few weeks expressed great surprise at the change in him. "He looks older, his face is pale, he seems very depressed and to feel keenly his retirement from the Admiralty." Churchill himself subsequently described the experience as the most painful in his life.

As might be expected, his own memoirs omit any handwringing. They contain a rather touching passage, however, that permits a strong inference. A few days before his departure he had a visit from Lord Kitchener, who was quite aware of Churchill's enormous contribution before the war in refurbishing the British navy so that it was fully prepared when hostilities finally broke out. "After some general remarks he asked me whether it was settled that I should leave the Admiralty. I said it was. He asked me what I was going to do. I said I had no idea, nothing was settled. He spoke very kindly about our work together. He evidently had no idea how narrowly he had escaped my fate. As he got up he turned and said, in the impressive and almost majestic manner which was natural to him, 'Well, there is one thing at any rate that they cannot take from you. The Fleet was ready.'" Churchill was deeply moved by "the rugged kindness and warm-hearted courtesy which led him to pay me this visit." His only stronger support came from his staunch and loving wife, his darling Clementine.

He remained a member of the government for about another six months, more particularly as a member of the Dardanelles Committee charged with continuing the Gallipoli campaign. But his status seems increasingly to have been that of hanger-on, with his influence waning into impotence. For a man of his talent and energy, it was an intolerable situation. He was relieved from it in November, when Asquith reconstituted the ineffectual committee into a smaller War Committee to which Churchill was not appointed.

The former First Lord of the Admiralty was now quite literally unemployed. Despite several applications to Asquith, he simply could not get a job in government at any respectable level. And so he decided to join his old regiment on the continent, despite his elegant mother's wails of despair at the thought of her splendid son's being relegated to the nitty-gritty of trench warfare. But he considered it, under the circumstances, a relegation devoutly to be wished.

His time in the ranks was short. In 1917 his admirer Lloyd George, who had succeeded Asquith as coalition prime minister, brought him back to the Cabinet as munitions minister, giving him the opportunity to introduce thousands of tanks to help break the stalemate on the western front. Although he remained in the government after the war and during most of the twenties, the thirties were a period of political exile and impotent frustration while he played Cassandra against the British apathy over the resurgence of German militarism. But with the outbreak of war in September 1939 he found himself once again First Lord of the Admiralty, and by May 1940 he had succeeded the hapless Neville Chamberlain as prime minister.

Adolph Hitler now had a worthy antagonist. Because of Hitler, Churchill became the most famous prime minister in British history. Never would so many owe so much to one man.

# Harry Truman
# and the
# Haberdashery

In the early 1920s, although Calvin Coolidge had not yet arrived to fix the phenomenon in the amber of his golden prose, the business of America was business. In that environment Harry S. Truman was a persistent loser. He seems even to have had that reputation early in life. When he was courting Bess, her mother was dismayed that Bess would consider him seriously. She evidently agreed with a friend who later reported that he "was just about the most unpromising prospect for a husband we had around here then."

Truman wanted to improve these prospects as quickly and as conspicuously as possible. Early in 1915, when he was thirty and eager to leave the drudgery of the family farm, he saw the goddess Opportunity beckoning when a city slicker named Jerry Culbertson offered him an interest in a lead and zinc mine near Commerce, Oklahoma, just south of the Kansas border. A visit to the town proved very persuasive, since it was full of the propitious bustle brought on by warring Europe's rising demand for the two metals. A mine in this area looked like a lead-and-zinc-pipe cinch.

Truman invested a precious $2,000 and months of weekend effort added to his work on the family farm. All to no avail; the mine yielded not an ounce of metal. Then word got around that *the* place for mining lead and zinc was about five miles to the northeast, near the town of Picher. Truman was asked to invest another $2,500, but he had nowhere near that amount available, nor could he raise it. Others could, however, and did, and their investments in the Picher area made them rich.

The next year an uncle died, leaving his own farm and his half interest in the family farm to the Truman family, which consisted of Harry, his widowed mother, and his brother and sister. Although this provided Harry with no more cash, it did put him in a better position to raise some, and soon thereafter Culbertson again appeared on his horizon with another great proposition. This time it was oil. Demand was bound to skyrocket, what with the war and the new internal combustion engine. It was a three-way deal, Culbertson explained, with each partner taking a third of the profits. David Morgan, an old hand in the oil business, would contribute 1,500 acres of promising land he owned in eastern Oklahoma; Culbertson would contribute his promotional know-how; and Truman would put in $5,000 in cash.

Truman had no cash, however, so he borrowed the money, in five notes for $1,000 each, all due in ten months. His partners expressed their confidence in his financial condition by insisting that his mother cosign the notes. This done, he became treasurer of the firm with Morgan as president and Culbertson as secretary, and the game began. For the company's first test well, Morgan went not to Oklahoma but to Louisiana, where he had leased a site adjacent to a Standard Oil well that had already proved itself a liquid-gold mine. He sank the test well and came up with what he called "some the finest salt water in the entire area." He had similar luck in Oklahoma. In Kansas in 1918 (after Truman had left for Europe, in uniform), Morgan drilled a well to 1,500 feet and then, discouraged, sold it with the lease to another company, which continued the drilling and struck oil at 2,400 feet. After that there "was never a dry hole found on that three hundred and twenty acres," Truman reported later. "It was the famous Tweeter Pool."

Meanwhile Culbertson had sold his third of the business, not to anyone's great surprise. When Truman returned from the army, the company was dissolved. Although it had not dragged anyone into bankruptcy, it had never done better than break even, and no one seemed sorry to see it go. Certainly Truman, who had been affluent (and frugal) enough as an artillery captain to put aside a little capital for postwar projects, was far from inconsolable. His thoughts were concentrated on two postwar projects, both enormously important to him.

First, he was determined to find some way to make a living other than farming. He had worked the family farm conscientiously and competently, but his heart had never been in it. His was not the classic case of the hayseed youngsters who were now returning after seeing Paris—"How are you gonna keep them down on the farm?" In 1919 he was thirty-five years old, and he had seen enough of Kansas City before the war to know that he was happier there than in the country. His second project, at least equally important to his future happiness, was to marry Bess. Which he did, in June.

After a brief honeymoon the couple moved in with Bess's mother and grandmother in her family's seven-bedroom house in Independence. A week or so later Truman happened to meet an army buddy in Kansas City, Eddie Jacobson. In such meetings reminiscing is mandatory, of course, and the two men spent some of the morning sharing memories of their days in the service. Many of those they had spent managing the regimental canteen at training camp. Under their management the canteen had proved a very profitable source of funds for the regimental kitty, which supported recreational and other morale-boosting activities. An idea was born. Why not pool their resources and experience? Why not open a store in Kansas City—a men's furnishings store, perhaps, since Jacobson had had considerable experience selling men's clothing on the road? With his knowledge of the merchandise, he could do the buying. Truman would keep the books. And they would both do the selling.

This meant raising capital; the initial investment in inventory alone would run about $35,000. Jacobson had enough savings to cover the larger portion, but Truman would have to come up with $15,000 for his share. He did so by selling his interest in the family farm to his mother, brother, and sister. Since this brought him $20,000, he was able to hedge his bet a little by buying an apartment in Kansas City for $5,000 and renting it out. The partners signed a lease for five years on a downtown store across the street from the famous Muehlebach Hotel. By the end of November they were ready for business. They opened their doors on the twenty-ninth and waited for the expected rush of customers.

They were not disappointed. Their store became something of a mecca for veterans eagerly changing to civvies and for war-prosperous civilians with surplus cash for silk shirts and underwear. Since "Captain Harry" had been a popular commander during the war, the Boys from Battery D became a lucrative rooting section. During 1920 the store turned over its inventory twice, bringing its owners an inspiringly comfortable return on their investment. The profits, minus their modest living expenses, all went back into the business, increasing and improving their stock. In addition to the money, they put in long hours, with the store open thirteen hours a day, from eight till nine, six days a week. It was as busy as a beehive, and as productive.

Then, in 1921, disaster arrived in the form of Warren G. Harding's "return to normalcy." Tariff increases, introduced to protect and encourage American manufacturing industries, wreaked havoc in the Corn Belt. Good harvests dropped the prices of the food that farmers had to sell, while the tariffs generally raised the prices of the tools they had to buy. The ensuing farm depression was a catastrophe not only for many farmers but also for the city merchants who relied heavily, if sometimes only indirectly, on their trade and their prosperity. Among these merchants were Harry Truman and Eddie Jacobson, who throughout 1921 had to mark down their merchandise continually to keep pace with the 40 percent drop in farm prices and the 50 percent drop in farm income. During that year in the United States three times as many merchants went bankrupt as in 1919. The estimated value of the Truman-Jacobson inventory dropped from $35,000 in January 1920 and 1921 to $10,000 in January 1922. Ironically, they had had an offer for the business early in 1921, a good offer based on the earlier estimates, and had turned it down.

They had no such offers in 1922. They found themselves borrowing from new creditors to pay off old creditors. In 1921 Truman had sold the Kansas City apartment for $5,000 to make a down payment on a farm priced at $13,800; now, to borrow $5,000 from a bank, he had to put up his equity in the farm as collateral. As this money disappeared into the pockets of creditors, the partners concluded that the business was dead and would have to be declared so. They hated the thought of filing for bankruptcy, however, and so they arranged with their creditors to return their remaining inventory and pay the balance of their debts on the installment plan. All told, Truman estimated that he had lost about $30,000 in the venture, including his original investment. But the partners paid every penny of their debts, although it took them ten uncomfortable years.

Three failures in business proved enough for Harry Truman. His chances could not be any worse in politics, in which he had always been interested anyway. An election for a county judgeship was to be held within a few months, and he decided to give it a whirl. One of his customers at the haberdashery was a fellow he had known in the service, a fellow whose family had some pretty good political connections, and Truman decided to ask him for help, or at least for advice. The fellow's name was Jim Pendergast.

Thirty years later Winston Churchill confessed to Harry Truman that he had had a very low opinion of Truman when the latter succeeded Franklin Roosevelt. But now, in 1952, he conceded, "I misjudged you badly. Since that time you, more than anyone else, have saved western civilization."

# Walt Disney and the Distributors

In 1919, at the age of seventeen, Walt Disney left Chicago, his hometown, for Kansas City. His aim was not so much to go to Kansas City as it was to get away from Chicago and especially from his job as bottle-washer and apple-masher at the jelly factory where his father was a supervisor. He had been to art school and, although he had shown no promise of displacing Picasso, he had learned enough to know that there were careers other than bottle-washing and apple-mashing.

The idea of drawing pictures for a living appealed to him. This preference was confirmed by his first job in Kansas City. In the fall a commercial art studio hired him as an apprentice to help with the growing Christmas rush. He sketched rough layouts, mostly for farm equipment ads, through most of October and November, after which the preholiday rush and the job expired together. He had earned a total of only $75 but had found the atmosphere congenial and the work enjoyable. He also had learned some practical shortcuts that had never been mentioned in art school.

After a few weeks of work in the local post office and another few weeks in a partnership with another illustrator, he found a job with a firm calling itself the Kansas City Film Ad Company. It made sixty-second animated cartoon movies to be shown as commercials in local movie houses. In making the movies it used cardboard cutouts rather than drawings. The illusion of movement was achieved by changing the positions of the limbs of the articulated dolls very slightly for each frame of film. Although the work offered little challenge for Disney's sketching talents, he was intrigued by the process, by its problems, and by the opportunities it offered for improvements. He found himself longing to experiment with the process in an effort to adapt it to actual cartoons, but the job offered no time for such sideline activities.

So he turned to moonlighting. He persuaded his boss to lend him a camera for experimenting at home in the evening. Over the next few months he managed to produce some very brief animated cartoons, called Laugh-O-Grams, for showing in a neighborhood theater. Before long he had sold enough of them to buy a camera and return the borrowed one, and then go into business for himself. He scrounged some capital and hired some employees, not for wages but for the opportunity to learn the business and the chance of sharing in the profits, if any.

The Laugh-O-Grams company became surprisingly productive. It soon created seven animated cartoons, each seven minutes long, based on fairy tales such as "Little Red Riding Hood" and "Puss 'n' Boots." Its New York disributor apparently did a brisk business leasing these films, but Laugh-O-Grams' percentage never found its way back to Kansas City. Disney, who had meanwhile started paying salaries out of the firm's capital, had to let everyone go. He gave up his apartment and lived in the office, sleeping on pillows spread on the floor. So much for Laugh-O-Grams.

Although his failure had been in distribution, not creation, he was nonetheless destitute. The next couple of years were pretty bleak. He managed to survive this period, he said later, only because he liked beans. For haircuts he traded cartoons, which the barber displayed in his window. With his movie camera, which he had somehow held on to, he took home movies of children for parents proud enough to pay his small fee. He wangled an occasional assignment as a newsreel stringer. He accepted money—cash from his brother Roy, who had a modest war pension and who was then recovering from tuberculosis in a veterans' hospital, and credit from a couple of restauranteurs in his neighborhood who could now and then rescue him from his diet of beans and bread.

He did produce two animated cartoons. One, commissioned by a dental institute, was called *Tommy Tucker's Tooth*. When Disney received a call from the liaison dentist, telling him that the job was funded and that he could come to his office to discuss the details, Disney had to explain that his only shoes were at a shoe repair store (from which he had returned unshod) and could the dentist please come to him. The dentist did. The other movie, *Alice in Cartoonland*, combined a live actress, a young girl playing Alice, with animated drawings. Although crudely done by his later standards, it was a novel idea, and the film did get shown. But he could not capitalize on it at the time.

In 1923 he decided that he would have to leave Kansas City and make a new start somewhere else. The most promising somewhere else seemed to be Hollywood. Reluctantly he sold his precious camera and made the rounds of his multitudinous creditors, offering partial settlement of his extensive debts. Most of them generously declined payment until he got back on his feet. And so that July, with a few articles of clothing in an imitation-leather suitcase and $40 in his pocket, he caught a train to the coast.

What he found in Hollywood was discouraging. This was a time of consolidation, with the myriad small studios of the earlier days gradually disappearing into the capacious maws of giants like Universal, MGM, and Paramount. It was not a time of golden opportunity for a young interloper eager to start up a new company. Disney, figuring that he was several years too late for that kind of venture, tried his luck at Universal. He knocked on many doors, some at the humblest levels, but no one responded with a job offer. Meanwhile he saw cartoon series like "Felix the

Cat" and "Krazy Kat" appearing more and more often on theater screens. He seemed to be watching a parade passing him by. And up.

Soon after he had decided, in desperation, to try starting up his own business after all and to revive his Laugh-O-Grams, a New York distributor named Charles Mintz offered him $1,500 apiece (just about the going rate) for a series of "Alice in Cartoonland" short subjects. Walt and brother Roy estimated that they could produce the films at a cost of $500 apiece, given some prodigious scrimping. What they needed was that first $500. Half of it they extracted from an unenthusiastic uncle, and the other half from somewhere that no one remembers. Sure enough, with that money they created the lead film, sent it to Mintz in New York, received their stipend, paid off the uncle and other creditors, and had a stake with which to start producing the series.

But Disney, increasingly dissatisfied with the films' technical imperfections after each was put in the can and shipped off to New York, began spending more money on sets and equipment and employees, so that costs rose steadily. Soon six films had been completed and sent east, but then Mintz came to Hollywood to report that Alice was not doing as well as expected, adding that he would like to terminate the contract. The brothers, who had just finished the seventh of the series, persuaded him to take it back to New York and give it a try. He did so, and it turned out to be not only the most deftly executed but also the most lucrative of all their work to date. Mintz, impressed, kept them under contract and even began raising the payment per film.

In early 1927, however, Mintz decided that "Alice" was showing signs of becoming an unprofitable bore. His brother-in-law, George Winkler, shortly thereafter appeared at the little Disney studio to ask Walt for a replacement. In response Disney proposed a series starring a rabbit—animators had long since given up portraying unmanageable humans in favor of more convincingly humanoid animals. He resisted naming the rabbit Peter despite the obvious connection. A drawing from a hat, appropriately, produced an acceptable name, and the new "Oswald the Rabbit" series was on its way.

To the delight of all concerned, Oswald proved more popular and profitable than Alice had ever been. The studio turned out a film each month, and almost every month Winkler came from New York to hand Disney a check and pick up the latest movie for his return. Occasionally some underling would perform this lowly chore, but these exceptions were so rare that the Disneys became a little uneasy. Winkler seemed to be making himself quite at home and very popular with some key employees.

His tactics became clear later that year when Disney traveled with his wife to New York partly for a vacation but mainly to renegotiate the studio's contract with distributor Mintz. Disney, who was now receiving $2,250 per film, asked for $2,500. He was offered $1,800. After recovering from the shock, he declined—and also learned what Winkler had been up to. Take it or leave it, he was told, but if you don't take it we'll hire away your best people and continue the "Oswald" series, since we hold the contract.

The dismayed Disney did not take it, and his friendly distributors carried out their threat. He had been city-slickered out of a valuable part of his staff and out of the cartoon series that had promised finally to bring him some substantial success, all before he could even catch a train home. At the station with his wife, although thoroughly depressed about his future, he wired Roy, "Everything okay, coming home," to keep him from worrying over the next several days. But he knew that everything was far from okay.

The train trip seems to have been just what he needed, offering relative solitude, the consolation and inspiration provided by his wife, and some time to think. When next he saw Roy, he was full of plans for a new series of cartoon shorts. The leading character would be a mouse. To be called Mortimer. No, not Mortimer. Mickey.

# Cole Porter and
## *See America First*

The public image of Cole Porter lived a life that Riley, Croesus and Louis XIV would have envied. A life positively glutted with health, wealth, and good fortune. Oh, there was that horseback-riding accident in the 1940s, but it did not incapacitate him or end his career. And his professional life was one of uninterrupted success. When Hollywood decided in 1946 to make a movie of his life—entitled *Night and Day* and starring Cary Grant as Porter—the story went that the problem would be to find a smidgen of tragedy, a touch of failure, to give the film some dramatic interest. But the problem was never really solved.

In his memoirs Porter denied the public image, especially the Panglossian view of his career. The motion picture, he complained, "had no resemblance to reality." He had, he conceded, written thirty-two musical comedies, of which twenty-four could be legitimately classified as hits, and had composed some fifteen hundred songs—music and lyrics—including some very standard "standards":

Always True to You in My Fashion
Anything Goes

152

Begin the Beguine
Blow, Gabriel, Blow
Can-Can
It's De-Lovely
Don't Fence Me In
I Get a Kick Out of You
In the Still of the Night
I've Got You Under My Skin
Love for Sale
My Heart Belongs to Daddy
Night and Day
Too Darn Hot
What is This Thing Called Love?
Why Can't You Behave?
Wunderbar
You Do Something to Me
You'd Be So Nice to Come Home to
You're the Top

He also had provided scores for eight movies, which brought him considerable fame, as well as a fortune that he did not need. He and Irving Berlin were, admittedly, the "deans of American popular music." Beyond that, he had even composed a classical ballet, *Within the Quota*, which, performed by a Swedish ballet company in Europe and America, had proved very successful if not memorable.

Nevertheless, he insisted that "for nine hard and miserable years [he] was the most outstanding failure in the musical world." The number of years may be doubtful—perhaps more like twelve than nine—and the misery may have seemed like luxurious comfort to anyone outside the world of Beautiful People, but his memory, as plumbed by his biographer Richard Hubler, made a good case for a long stretch of failure. Year after year, he reported, his early efforts were summarily rejected by producers, some of whom went out of their way to discourage him. Charles Dillingham found his music loathsome, and Florenz Ziegfeld generously informed him that his "attempts at music are either ridiculous or disgusting."

His blue, if not black, period seems to have started in 1916 with the New York production of *See America First*. He wrote the music to a libretto written by a friend he had met during his abortive academic stopover at the Harvard Law School, T.L. Riggs. They shared writing the lyrics. The production, despite its high cost and its starring of Clifton Webb in the lead, lasted only three weeks and evoked a stream of unmitigated critical derision. One critic, noting a report that the musical's two authors were from out of town, urged them "to return to wherever they came from and stay there." Riggs, thoroughly defeated, gave up musical comedy for life. Converting to Roman Catholicism, he was ordained a priest and wound up as the chaplain at Yale. Porter was disheartened enough to go overseas and join the Foreign Legion. But he did take along a small, portable piano, which he carried strapped to his back, enabling him to respond immediately to any requests for musical entertainment. In Paris, where he ended up at the close of World War I, he met Linda Lee Thomas, his future wife and most ardent, supportive fan.

On shipboard, on his return trip to New York, a fellow passenger turned out to be Raymond Hitchcock, a celebrated comedian in American musical revues. Late one night, at the piano in the main dining room, Porter played and sang a number of his songs for Hitchcock. After listening to them all with total impassivity, Hitchcock offered to consider every one of them for his new production, *Hitchy-Koo of 1919*. On their arrival in New York he went further, introducing Porter to Max Dreyfus, a music publisher and discoverer of Vincent Youmans, Jerome Kern, and George Gershwin—and now of Cole Porter, although it would be a while before the discovery took on any significance.

*Hitchy-Koo*, whether because or in spite of its title, was an immediate hit, running for two years, but Porter's songs failed to attract any favorable attention—with one exception. One day before the show was scheduled to open, Florenz Ziegfeld called

Charles Dillingham, who somewhat ironically was the producer of the Hitchcock revue, offering "some old flower costumes" that had ended up as surplus in that year's Follies. Dillingham accepted them and Hitchcock asked Porter for a song to match. The next day the young music man came up with "Old Fashioned Garden," but, to Porter's dismay, it was not included in the show until later, when something was needed to occupy a gap in the action. Thereafter the tune and the costumes made up the most popular part of the show. "Old Fashioned Garden" eventually netted Porter $100,000 in royalties. (It failed, incidentally, in England, where gardening is a universal preoccupation, because it brought together a variety of incompatible flowers. Porter was no botanist.)

The song's popularity failed to bring any offers. Porter again fled to Europe. That December, in Paris, he and Linda were married and settled down to some serious party-giving there and on the Riviera to a guest list that included over the years Anita Loos, Sergi Diaghilev, F. Scott Fitzgerald, Irving Berlin, Mary Garden, Artur Rubinstein, Igor Stravinsky, Grace Moore, Vincent Youmans, Pablo Picasso, George Gershwin, Noël Coward, Moss Hart, Fannie Brice, Beatrice Lillie, Douglas Fairbanks, Mary Pickford, and the Prince of Wales. Given the frenzied social life that such a list suggests, it is astonishing that Porter managed to write anything. But he did, returning to New York periodically to submit his work to every producer whom he could get to listen. Many listened, and all shook their heads. Too serious, too highbrow, they told him, and anyway there's a prejudice against expatriate artists of any kind.

In the spring of 1921, however, Hitchcock cabled him that he'd like some music for a new Hitchy-Koo planned for that year. Porter eagerly wrote the score only to discover, when the revue opened in Philadelphia, that all but two of his twenty-four songs had been eliminated. The two retained were, naturally, the least distinguished of the lot and failed to bring him any notice at all. So he and Linda went back to Europe, this time for an extensive tour of France, and then to Italy and Sicily. From Sicily they went to

Egypt for an eight-week cruise on the Nile. Porter hired a crew consisting of actors, dancers, and musicians so that he could stage an impromtu show wherever they stopped.

A couple of years later, in 1924, he received an offer to compose the score for the *Greenwish Village Follies*, but once again all but two of his songs were eliminated from the production. This time he returned to Europe (he wrote in his memoirs) "to alternate fits of entertaining and despondency, studying music and history trying to get [himself] out of a black mood of despair." He and Linda toured Spain. They went to the opera in Milan and in every other Italian town boasting an opera house (and often found the performance better than at La Scala). Porter "did everything and anything, from Egyptology to mah-jongg, to forget composition." But he never stopped studying music.

One day in 1928, as he was sitting on the sands of a beach looking out over the Adriatic Sea, a producer named E. Ray Goetz approached him with a suggestion that he might write the score for a Broadway revue that Goetz had in mind. Porter responded with his inevitably eager affirmative, and this time his music not only was accepted but was actually included in the show, which was a deeply gratifying hit. From that time on, his music would be in demand and, as he said later, he "was never again really in the doldrums."

# Billy Mitchell and the Wild Blue Yonder

O ne problem with not being able to suffer fools gladly is that they are not always fools. More often than not, perhaps, but not always. William "Billy" Mitchell, progenitor of the United States Air Force, had this inability and the attendant problem. Success, at least in the sense of spectacular vindication of his fervently held views, was largely posthumous.

Success in another and more conventional sense came to him early in his career. In 1912, at the age of twenty-two, he was already on the U.S. Army's General Staff, its youngest officer. After learning to fly in 1916, he was given command of the Army's miniscule aviation group. During World War I, besides flying combat missions, he became air commander for successively larger army groups. He emerged from the war a hero, a celebrity, a brigadier general, and the prime candidate for the post of chief of Air Service. His appointment as assistant chief marked the turning of his career into a struggle steeped in controversy and bitter disappointment.

Air power, he argued strenuously, was far too important, or soon

157

would be, to play handmaiden to the army and navy. It must be exercised by an independent military service, separately—and generously—funded. The overall responsibility for the national security should be vested in a new Department of Defense made up of army, navy and air force. But his proposal met with stony opposition not only from the brass hat establishment as a whole but, more significantly, from its most important representative, a soldier who outranked him in both military grade and heroic celebrity, General of the Army John "Blackjack" Pershing.

Meanwhile, however, Congress had become interested. In April 1919 it learned that the Secretary of War, Newton D. Baker, had assigned an assistant, Benedict Crowell, to form a committee to investigate the air power problem and come up with a recommendation. The committee, consisting of Crowell, a couple of army colonels, a navy captain, and three representatives of aircraft manufacturing firms, submitted their report and recommendation in June. It thereupon disappeared into the bureaucratic maw and might never have been heard from again but for some leaks and the bird dog instincts of the chairman of the aviation subcommittee of the House Committee on Military Affairs, New York's Representative Fiorello LaGuardia, the future mayor and "Little Flower." In December Crowell testified before his subcommittee that Secretary Baker had added a note to the report disagreeing with its conclusion and then had buried the report in the departmental files. And what was the report's conclusion? That the government's "air activities" should be included in a single department on an equal footing with the army and navy.

The hearings, which lasted two months and included a great deal of testimony from Mitchell and many others on both sides, brought the air power controversy forcefully to the attention of Congress and the public. Mitchell's testimony also created considerable resentment against him in the highest of the gold braid echelons, since he had committed the ultimate treason of appealing to the civilian authority. But it also stiffened congressional spines against the navy's efforts, during 1920, to cancel or neutralize a proposed trial of air bombardment's effects on naval vessels. Some admirals were worried by the prospect of any such trial, although many others were confident that the trial would demonstrate naval indestructibility. You can't, said one, kill a hippopotamus with mosquitoes. Secretary of the Navy Josephus Daniels announced that he would be willing to stand on the bridge of a vessel while it was being bombed.

He did not repeat this offer after the first air attacks were conducted during the trial, sinking a destroyer and cruiser in Chesapeake Bay. Nor on the final day of the trial in July 1921, when the target was to be a German battleship scheduled for destruction by treaty. Daniels, although not confident enough for bridge duty, had assigned the battleship *Pennsylvania* to be ready to finish off the German vessel after the air bombardment failed. After all, the *Ostfriesland* was protected by 27,000 tons of hardened steel, with eighty-five watertight compartments encased in a triple hull. She had taken eighteen hits from twelve- and fourteen-inch shells at Jutland, and another from a mine, and had steamed away under her own indomitable power. Even the *Pennsylvania* might have a hard time of it. But Billy Mitchell and the Provisional Air Brigade, with their 2,000 pound bombs, sighted the *Ostfriesland* and sank same.

They put on a similar show in another trial later that year, and again in 1923, sinking a total of three old but heavily armored battlewagons. The tests proved conclusively that the battleship was vulnerable, but Mitchell, caught up in his own enthusiasm, declared it totally obsolete. In a country thoroughly disillusioned by the great war to save the world for democracy, money for defense was being measured out in teaspoons, and Mitchell made quite a case, in aviation journals and popular magazines, for concentrating available funds on the hundred of planes that could be provided at the cost of a single battleship. He was deeply disappointed that this was not done immediately, but his disappointment was nothing compared to the consternation in the halls of brass. Alarmed admirals and generals buried their jealousies in the common cause, and Mitchell soon found himself in Europe, on a tour of inspection. Six months after his return he was inspecting the Pacific and the Orient. On the latter tour, even though it was also a honeymoon trip for him and his new bride, he could not resist making some waves. In Hawaii, he reported, the army and navy commanders were not on speaking terms and therefore had developed separate, uncoordinated plans for defense of the islands, leaving Hawaii wide open to an attack (he warned) by an aggressive naval power like Japan.

On his return from the Pacific tour in July 1924 he reentered the lists with unrepentant gusto, tilting against the fuddy-duddy strongholds through magazine articles and at congressional hearings. In the following spring he lost his temporary grade of brigadier general and his job as assistant chief of Air Service. Shortly thereafter Colonel Mitchell was transferred out of Washington to a minor post in San Antonio, Texas. To his adversaries in the navy, San Antonio must have seemed as remote as Antarctica, but it was not too remote for him to learn of, and react to, their next big blunder.

In September the navy undertook a couple of promotional stunts to persuade the American public that the old sea dogs knew what they were about. To counter the army's around-the-world flight in 1924, they announced a nonstop flight of three seaplanes from San Francisco to Honolulu. In addition, the monster Zeppelin dirigible *Shenandoah* would make a 3,000-mile trip inland, showing itself at state fairs in Ohio, Iowa, Minnesota, Wisconsin, and Michigan. The combination would give the navy, in the public's eye, a kind of spectacular ubiquity.

That first week in September was indeed spectacular, but not as planned. On September first the navy had to announce that one of the seaplanes had come down with engine trouble, although the other two had left for Hawaii. On the second it had to report that one of the planes was wallowing in the sea about 300 miles offshore and that the other was missing. (It was found later, also wallowing.) On the fourth it had to report that the *Shenandoah*, only twelve hours out, had crashed in a severe storm in Ohio with the loss of fourteen crewmen, including the skipper (who had protested the inland trip as unfamiliar and dangerous). And on the sixth it had to read a public statement by Mitchell, prepared "after mature deliberation," blaming the accident on "the incompetency, criminal negligence, and almost treasonable administration of the national defense by the War and Navy Departments." Since the closest thing to homage in this statement was the word "almost," he was immediately summoned to Washington to appear before a court-martial on a charge of violating the catchall 96th Article of War, which forbids "all conduct of a nature to bring discredit upon the military service." That he had been guilty of such conduct (like others not so charged) was obvious, and this was the only thing that the court was empowered to determine under the article. And so he was found guilty and sentenced to a five-year suspension of rank and duty. A month later, on the first day of February 1926, he resigned from the army.

He continued the battle in his lectures and writing, including repeated warnings against the Japanese militarists "working almost with desperation" toward ridding the Pacific of American naval power. But Americans generally were losing interest in his cause, preoccupied as they were with the good life of the late 1920s. When the bubble broke in 1929 and a Democrat took over the White House in 1932, Mitchell's hopes rose, since he had worked hard for the party during the campaign. The Air Service recently had become the Army Air Corps, with more autonomy and prestige, and Mitchell was widely expected to be named assistant secretary of war for Air Service. But Franklin Roosevelt, whose naval background may have made him susceptible to navy influence, did not do the expected.

Americans were now preoccupied with something more urgent than the good life. As the great depression deepened, Billy Mitchell suffered the most painful of fates to be visited on a prophet in his own country. He became a bore. Rejection letters from publishers began arriving in his mail. Readers, they said, were no longer interested. They had other problems.

He took it hard. If he had been better at relaxing, he might have lived to a comfortable old age well beyond his days of vindication. But he died in February 1936, in his middle fifties, too soon to see the spectacular demonstration of air power over the following thirty months or so, in Spain. And that, of course, was only the beginning.

# Clark Gable and His Broadway Doldrums

T he young Clark Gable was a smash in Houston. In 1927 his first wife and first agent, Josephine Dillon, had arranged for him to join a stock company in that city to give him some badly needed experience in the craft to which he was now totally committed. The company was thriving, staging a different play each week in Houston's Palace Theater, and paying very respectable salaries for those times.

Gable stayed with the company for about nine months. During the first three he played second lead, for $75 a week, but when the leading man dropped out he was given the lead roles at $200 a week. The first of these was that of the tough Irish sailor Mat Burke in Eugene O'Neill's *Anna Christie*. Beautifully suited to it, he became a Houston star overnight. The next six months were a time of matinee idol celebrity, complete with autograph beggars, giggling teenage girls, and lovelorn matrons.

Meanwhile Josephine Dillon had gone to New York seeking a good role for Gable among producers of her acquaintance. She was sincerely determined to promote his career, but an earlier visit to

Houston may have given her some additional incentive to move her husband to New York, since she suspected a possible liaison with an affluent widow named Ria Langham. One of her producer friends did have a good part for him, in a play called *Machinal* starring a popular actress of the time, Zita Johann. Gable was delighted to receive a summons to Broadway. "All my life I had been waiting for the chance," he remarked later, "just to plant my feet on the sidewalks that all actors have walked at some time." But when he joined Dillon in New York, the tension between them erupted into an open and permanent break, whereupon she returned to California.

Gable threw himself into the rehearsals. Zita Johann, to whom he had been described as "a Woolworth Romeo," found him a splendid supporting actor—professional, unflappable, industrious, conscientious—although she was one leading lady who could keep their relationship platonic. She acknowledged that he had "impact," but not particularly for her. She considered him "genial" and "affable"—and, interestingly, "bemused." One thing she remembered about him most vividly was his sitting in front of the mirror in his dressing room before each performance, busily applying white paint to his two gold teeth.

*Machinal* opened on Broadway in September 1928 to very favorable notices, including a few briefly complimentary comments on Gable, one of which described him, prophetically, as "vigorous and brutally masculine." He stayed with the play for three months, until it finally had to make way for the premiere of *Holiday*. Suddenly he was unemployed, without a Josephine Dillon to plug his talents. Ria Langham had joined him in New York and was there to provide moral and other support, but she was in no position to market his talents. Although he was never in any danger of growing threadbare in this dismal period—indeed, with Ria's help and guidance, he greatly improved in dress and manner—he had to join the perennial hopefuls in making the grueling, frustrating, humiliating rounds of producers' offices. Outwardly buoyant, he revealed only to Ria how deeply depressed he was by persistent rejections.

He found himself painfully remembering the strongly articulated opinion of this father—a tough oil wildcatter to whom acting was for sissies—that he would never amount to anything. Gable told Ria he thought his father was right and that Gable should give it all up and open a men's clothing store.

But he continued making the rounds, and in the early summer of 1929 he got a part. It was a good part, the lead in *Gambling*, a play being produced by George M. Cohan. The production opened that fall in Philadelphia, but something happened to Gable on its way to New York. He may simply have fallen victim to Cohan's discomfort with his own behind-the-scenes role. Soon after the opening Cohan began rewriting the play with himself in the lead, and a few weeks later Gable found himself out in the street again.

To aggravate his resulting depression, there was the economic depression. His meager investments were swept away in the historic crash. He was hired for a play entitled *Hawk Island*, but he had so few illusions about it that, every day during its four-week run, he continued making the rounds of producers' offices. His efforts got him a small part in a play that quickly closed out of town, and then another minor role in another play that ran for eight barely noticed weeks on Broadway in the spring of 1930.

But someone had noticed. Lillian Albertson, who produced and directed popular plays in Los Angeles with her husband, Louis MacLoon, had been watching his career as best she could from such a distance. Three years earlier she had directed him in a play and had been impressed not so much by his actual performance as by his potential. In selecting plays for production she had not forgotten him, and now she believed that she really had something for him in *The Last Mile*, a current Broadway success to which she had bought the rights for a production on the west coast. The story was about a group of Death Row prison inmates who try to escape, and the part she had in mind for Gable was the starring role, the group's leader, Killer Mears.

In the Broadway production the part was being played by

Spencer Tracy. Gable and Ria, now married, went to see it, returning home with Gable paralyzed by discouragement. Thoroughly unnerved by the obvious demands of the role and by Tracy's spectacular performance, he refused to have anything to do with *The Last Mile*. Over the next few days, however, Ria and the MacLoons used all their powers of persuasion. Finally, with great reluctance and tredpidation, Gable signed on.

In San Francisco the play was a flop. Not a disaster, but unnoticed, a nonevent. In June 1930 it opened at the Belasco Theater in Los Angeles and was an instant smash. For Gable it was Houston all over again, in spades. As Killer Mears he was tough, mean, menacing, almost bestial, and apparently mesmerizing. Suddenly he had a Los Angeles agent, Minna Wallis (sister of Hal Wallis and a well-connected hustler), and his Broadway agent was busily collecting parts for him to consider for his return to New York. Gable was looking forward to that return and to really establishing himself on the street where he had pounded so many pavements. All about him Hollywood was sizzling with feverish activity, suffering from a nervous condition brought on by the changeover to talking pictures. Studios were excitedly seeking actors who had demonstrated a possession of resonant vocal chords on the stage, but Gable, who had little experience in silent movies, as well as in the theater, showed no interest in anything but Broadway.

Minna Wallis, undismayed by his indifference, got him a part in a movie, a talking western in which, among other things, he would have to ride a horse. He said she was crazy—he had "never been *near* a horse, let alone *on* one!" But, after two weeks of intensive training, he was riding as though he had been born and raised in the saddle. One of the first things he was taught to do, through a sink-or-swim technique, was to take the horse hurtling downhill without getting thrown. Shortly after shooting started on the movie, the trainer got a wire from him: "The first thing I had to do was ride down a hill fast. Got away with it okay. Thanks, kid."

From then on, he got away with just about everything okay.

# Laurence Olivier and *Journey's End*

During the summer and fall of 1928 Laurence Olivier was living a life of uneasy ease. The ease was provided by a comfortable, and comfortably major, part in a long-running play, *Bird in Hand*, and by his leading lady, Jill Esmond Moore, with whom he was in love, who had accepted his proposal of marriage, and whose mother, a successful actress and producer, had invited him to stay with them in their country home. The uneasiness, the self-questioning amid the lotus eating, came from his own ambition, his restlessness in an undemanding role of lovesick young swain, his eagerness to get on with his career. Like most committed young actors, he longed for The Big Break, the vehicle that would make him a star overnight. But in his particular case the irony was that when it came, when it all but gripped his arm and tugged at his lapel, he failed to recognize it.

One evening, shortly before a performance of *Bird in Hand*, word spread about backstage that Basil Dean was in the audience. Dean was a controversial but celebrated theatrical producer and impresario, and everyone in the cast, including and perhaps especially Olivier, reacted accordingly, talent at the ready, all keyed up to the sticking point. He knew that Dean was planning a lavish production of *Beau Geste,* with Madeleine Carroll, and the prospect was enough to make an aspiring thespian's throat dry and mouth water simultaneously. Yet, although he gave it his all that night, he was devastated to learn that Dean had been overheard saying, "That beetly-browed boy's no good at all."

Nevertheless, several discouraging months later Dean rather desperately called him in for an interview, to which Olivier came with renewed hope and plucked eyebrows. Several weeks went by without an offer, although in December he was invited to come for a reading. Dean obviously was interested in him but was hoping for someone better. Meanwhile Olivier, to prove to Dean that *he* was that someone better, signed up to play in an essentially amateur production of R.C. Sherriff's *Journey's End.*

The history of *Journey's End* is itself a story of fate snatching success from the jaws of failure. Sherriff was a not very successful insurance agent with a talent for creating unmarketable plays. *Journey's End,* his seventh, had been unanimously rejected by London producers and many established actors, partly because it was a play about the war, especially a play without a single romantic scene, and even without a woman in the cast. Olivier had no illusions about the play's prospects but was willing to put in the three weeks of rehearsal for the two scheduled performances because he knew that Dean would be there to see him playing not a romantic lead but Captain Stanhope, the hard-bitten, hard-drinking, deteriorating company commander. His gamble, he hoped, would prove to be a profitable piece of moonlighting. And it did fulfill that hope in a way. Not long after seeing Olivier in the two performances that December, Dean offered him the role of Beau opposite Madeleine Carroll.

*Beau Geste* opened late in January 1929. Although it had been a highly successful silent movie with Ronald Colman, on the stage, and under Dean's flamboyant direction, it made a spectacle of itself. The special effects required for staging a realistic battle,

including a Maxim gun blasting away, as well as a Götterdäm-
merung type of funeral for the dead Beau, bordered on the
ludicrous and overwhelmed whatever dramatic quality the play
might have had. As a result the production was a critical and
popular catastrophe. And Olivier's notices were lukewarm, much
less favorable than those for a slightly younger colleague, Jack
Hawkins.

After four disappointing weeks Dean withdrew *Beau Geste*,
replacing it with a pseudo-Oriental spectacle, *The Circle of Chalk*.
Olivier played the male lead, a Chinese prince in love with a tea
house girl who is sold into slavery. Opening night was one of the
most miserable evenings in Olivier's life. The Chinese girl was
Anna May Wong, who had done well in silent movies but whose
broad California accent quickly dispelled any Oriental flavor that
might have been detectable in *The Circle*. Olivier's voice, however
impeccable his accent, was suffering the aftereffects of an attack of
laryngitis, and his solo song was punctuated by uncontrollable
leaps into the falsetto range. The machinery for rotating the
scenery turntable jammed, and the evening culminated in un-
planned spectacle when a stumble by a couple of bit players
pulling a rickshaw spilled the rickshaw's passenger, a stout
mandarin, across the footlights and into the orchestra. The play ran
only briefly.

And so it went for about the next year and a half. Olivier seemed
to have developed a kind of reverse Midas's touch, turning gold into
dross with every gesture. A comedy in which he joined Herbert
Marshall and Edna Best earned critical comment ranging from
"tedious" to "unendurable." After three more critical failures, he
played the lead in a play acclaimed by the critics but utterly ignored
by the public. In August he sailed to New York to appear in the
Broadway production of *Murder on the Second Floor*, which had
been a hit in London. Although it received fair notices, it played
only five weeks to tepidly responsive houses. No other work was
available to Olivier in New York, since foreign actors were limited to
one role per six-month period by American Equity rules.

Back in London it was not until December that he was offered another role, again in a play that failed dismally, although his own notices were generally favorable. He was beginning to be known among some critics as a loser, a competent actor struggling hopelessly against a malign fate. The first half of 1930 continued in this vein, without a single professional stage appearance. He was engaged for one performance in an amateur production and for minor roles in two English talking pictures—so-called quickies ground out to meet the requirements of the British Quota Act, under which a certain number of British-made films had to be produced to balance the imports from Hollywood. The movies were *The Temporary Widow* and *Too Many Cooks* and they were forgotten as quickly as they were made.

Meanwhile things had been going much differently for the cast of *Journey's End*. Everyone but Olivier had stuck with it, refusing offers for other roles and even trying to form a corporation to raise enough money for a commercial production. They were finally about to give up when a maverick producer with a deliciously rich friend suddenly appeared on the horizon, and the play opened in London in mid-January 1929, just a week before the lamentable advent of *Beau Geste*. It was received with nineteen curtain calls that evening and unanimously enthusiastic reviews the next morning. It ran for nearly 600 performances. Before the year was out it had appeared all over the world, in twenty-seven languages. It was a smash on Broadway and, later, a hit movie. And the young actor named Colin Clive, who had replaced Olivier in the Stanhope role (at the urging of another cast member, Maurice Evans), had become a star overnight.

By now, in the early summer of 1930, Olivier, having experienced some modest success so early in *Bird in Hand*, was losing hope of ever regaining momentum. He felt his burden of failure so heavily that when Noël Coward offered him the part of the husband in *Private Lives*, he turned it down. The play, he felt, was essentially a showpiece for the two leads, Coward himself and Gertrude Lawrence. A supporting role in the shadow of these two scintillating performers might prove his histrionic deathblow. He resisted, but Coward persisted, reminding him that this play was likely to be a success, something he needed badly after his run of turkeys. Further, the salary was fifty pounds a week, a respectable sum not to be scoffed at by a young man on the brink of matrimony. Olivier accepted, and he and Jill were married in July.

*Private Lives* was the making of him. Acting with Coward gave him priceless training, but the play was an enormous hit as well, bringing Olivier to the attention of London's most sophisticated theatergoers. Furthermore, after three months of full houses, the restless Coward rather impulsively took the show to New York in the fall (with Jill taking over the female role opposite Olivier, the original player having become inconveniently pregnant). The play took Broadway by storm, with the theater full of agents from Hollywood studios in search of talent with promising looks and, especially now, promising voices. Olivier had a splendid voice, well modulated and superbly controlled.

By the following spring, in 1931, he was in Hollywood.

# Humphrey Bogart and the Wood Splinter

"The young man," wrote the reviewer, "was what might mercifully be described as inadequate." The reviewer was one of New York's most influential critics, Alexander Woollcott. The young actor, or whatever, was Humphrey Bogart. And the year was 1923.

It was the twenty-four-year-old Bogart's second appearance on the stage. In the first he had played a Japanese houseboy with only one line, and he had been excruciating. In this second play, although in a more substantial and suitable role, he evidently was not much better. On opening night he was so badly dehydrated with jitters that during the first act he abruptly disappeared into the wings to get a drink of water, leaving the star, Neil Hamilton, to improvise as best he could. The play closed after only a few performances.

Next, however, came a hit. Starring Mary Boland and Clifton Webb, *Meet the Wife* ran for seven months. Bogart had a good part as a newsman and, except for rare instances of hangover catatonia, played it well enough not to be fired. But he never did seem to rise

172

much above that level. For years the roller-coaster line of his ups and downs, in terms of audience appreciation and critical reaction, ran quite consistently near the bottom of the chart. There were times when, to stay in the business and continue eating, he took jobs as stage manager. He was no star at this, either. Indeed, he got to know his first-wife-to-be well only after some of the scenery had fallen on her. Soon thereafter he gave up stage managing.

Yet his acting remained notably undistinguished, partly because his roles were generally undistinguished, limited mostly to "Tennis, anyone?" romantic bits. At a bar he frequented on 52nd Street he was the butt of a great deal of ribald comment from well-lubricated literati like Alexander Woollcott, Heywood Broun, Mark Hellinger and Dorothy Parker. The ribbing did not hurt him—since he was usually in no condition to feel much pain—as much as it angered him into resolving to learn more about his craft. Whether he did so at that time is not a matter of record, but his career languished during the rest of the tintinnabulating twenties, punctuated chiefly by a first marriage, to an actress, which consisted mostly of eighteen months of estrangement facilitated by thousands of miles of separation due to stage commitments. Within a year after the divorce he was married again, to another actress, for a somewhat longer and more satisfactory run.

Then came the 1929 Hollywood raid on Broadway which, over the next two or three years, was to translate so many able-bodied voices from the stage to the new talkies. In Bogart's case, however, the part he had been promised was given to Charles Farrell, with Bogart relegated to the off-screen role of giving Farrell voice lessons. Although he was being paid more than he had ever earned on Broadway ($750 a week, at a time when bread was about 10¢ a loaf and new cars could be bought for a few hundred dollars), Bogart quickly grew restive, but he was saved from doing anything rash by an offer of a bit part in a movie. Over the next couple of years he appeared in eight films starring, among others, Victor McLaglen, Spencer Tracy, Bette Davis, and Joan Blondell. At the end of this period he was receiving tenth billing. And then the moguls in charge of his fate decided to drop him because he wasn't getting anywhere and obviously never would get anywhere. Not in the movies, anyway.

In 1918, shortly before the Armistice, he had been a sailor on duty aboard the *Leviathan,* a huge liner then being used as a troop transport. On perhaps his seventeenth crossing of the Atlantic a U-boat shelled the liner, and in one too-close-for-comfort explosion his upper lip was pierced by a wooden splinter. Although the naval surgeon on duty sewed the lip as expertly as circumstances would permit, Bogart was left with the tight-lipped expression and the faint lisp that later became his trademarks. Now in 1932, these peculiarities did him in. They might not be important on the stage, where an actor is yards away from even the first row. But in the movies, in which a face could fill the screen and a voice could fill the theater, such defects would be murder. So said the moguls as they gave Bogart his walking papers. He returned to New York with some hope that his movie roles might open some doors for him on Broadway, maybe even get him a good part in a good play.

He could not have been more mistaken. Broadway was in the grip of the Great Depression. He did get some parts—in four plays, for which he rehearsed a total of five months only to see every one of them close in a week or less. On the evening of March 4, 1933, he opened in a play just hours before Franklin Roosevelt had closed the nation's banks. The audience consisted of ten people. The play lasted about a week, netting a grand total of some fifty dollars. He and his then wife, Helen Menken, gradually ran out of work as Broadway came almost to a standstill (of 152 plays put on that year, 121 were flops). His formerly affluent family could no longer be of any help—his father, a well-to-do physician, had lost nearly everything in the crash, and now patients were increasingly unable to pay their bills. The young couple lived in a shabby flat in a shabby section of the East Side, and the best job that Bogart could scare up was at an arcade, where he took on all comers at chess for a dollar a game. Fortunately he was a better than average chess player, but the games were too slow and the takers too few to buy him a house on Easy Street.

In September 1934 his physician father died, and the son assumed debts of about $10,000 that had accumulated in recent years, together with some $35,000 in uncollectable bills. His situation was pretty desperate, and so was his mood. He did get a part, however, in another forgettable drama that carried him long enough for him to reach his Big Break.

Arthur Hopkins, a Broadway producer, was scouting around for someone to play a gangster named Duke Mantee in Robert E. Sherwood's *The Petrified Forest*. Bogart called his office and asked for an audition. The next day in the theater, after Bogart had read for the part, Sherwood told Hopkins that he could not handle it, although he might be suitable for another role. But Leslie Howard, who was slated for the romantic lead, was impressed by the sardonic twang in that voice. This, he insisted, was the man for the part. He promised to work with him, to shape him into the part if necessary, but he had to have that voice.

The play was a great success from opening night onward. Bogart was too. The critics seemed to be seeing him for the first time— and indeed it was the first time that anyone had ever seen him in a part calling for a three-days' growth of stubble on his chin. Even Alexander Woollcott joined in the general praise. And the role earned Bogart enough money to pay all his debts and his father's, and to revive a special "F.Y." fund, as he called it, which he liked to keep as insurance against having to take a part that he could not stomach.

When the Warner brothers bought *The Petrified Forest* for Hollywood, they hired Leslie Howard for the romantic lead and arranged an option for Bogart to play Duke Mantee. Although Bogart interpreted this as a commitment, he and his wife got off the train in Los Angeles to be told that he had been replaced by Edward G. Robinson. Crestfallen, he nearly returned to New York in disgust. But he recalled a promise that Howard had made to him while they were together on Broadway. If the play were ever made into a movie Bogart would play Mantee. He cabled Howard, who was on vacation in Scotland. Howard responded by cabling the Warners that if they wanted him in the picture, Bogart would have to be given the part of Mantee. Still anxious over that stiff upper lip and atrocious lisp, the moguls put him through fifteen tests. But in the end they did give him the part.

Many years later, when he and his fourth wife, Lauren Bacall, had a daughter, they named her after Leslie Howard.

# Mao Tse-tung and the Twenty-Eight Bolsheviks

In 1930 the province of Kiangsi in southeastern China (geographically located in about the position that Tennessee occupies in the United States) was the prime stronghold of the Chinese Communist Party. In the party leadership Mao Tse-tung was first among rivals. But in that year two events occurred that presaged his downfall.

One was political. A collection of Chinese Communists had returned from a long period of intensive training in the Soviet Union, where they had won favor with Stalin by supporting him against the Trotsky dissidents. On their return to China in 1930, their leader issued a pamphlet calling for the "Bolshevizing" of the party, and from this straightforward proposal the group came to be known as the Twenty-Eight Bolsheviks. By Mao's relatively pragmatic standards they were ideological visionaries who might well inadvertently sacrifice the revolution on the altar of doctrinal purity, as in their proposal to concentrate efforts on the industrial proletariat in an overwhelmingly agricultural country. But they had strong outside support for political infighting and by early 1931

177

had taken control of the party, to Mao's considerable chagrin.

The other event was military. Chiang Kai-shek, alarmed by the accumulation of Red military power in "the Kiangsi soviet," began a campaign in late 1930 aimed at a final solution of the problem by eliminating the party's army through "encirclement and annihilation." In the first campaign he tried to encircle the major Red army units in Kiangsi with 100,000 Kuomintang troops, outnumbering the Communists by three to one. He was defeated, however, by the tactics that Mao characteristically employed against superior forces. By falling back and allowing the enemy advance units to spread out and separate, he could lure them individually into traps. His troops could then do the encircling, destroying each isolated unit as an effective fighting force. After these tactics had repulsed Chiang's assault, Mao eagerly sought to pursue "The Flying General" (his sobriquet in one of his poems for the continually airborne Chiang), but his recommendations failed to get the approval of the squabbling party chiefs and the Kuomintang army was allowed to withdraw relatively intact. To that injury the Twenty-Eight Bolsheviks added a measure of insult by shouldering Mao out of the Central Bureau. Without a voice in that potent assemblage, Mao found himself relegated more and more to the military sidelines.

Meanwhile The Flying General had been gathering together 200,000 well-equipped troops to have another go at his Kiangsi adversaries. He attacked in the spring but was again thrown back by Red troops using Mao's divide-and-conquer tactics. This time, indeed, his retreat seems to have been more general and precipitous. In a poem on the campaign Mao described the Red troops as marching 250 miles and "rolling the enemy back like a mat."

The frustrated Chiang waited only about a month to launch a third campaign, this time with 300,000 troops. Evidently he was a slow learner. He pushed his vanguards rapidly against the defenders, who chewed them up as efficiently as they had in the earlier attacks. In addition to their effective tactics, the Communists fought with underdog desperation, so that, when the Kuo-mintang army retreated again, in October, a Red general remarked to Mao that all the fat soldiers had worn themselves thin and the thin ones had worn themselves to death.

During the fighting that summer of 1931 the party's Central Committee in Shanghai, feeling unnecessarily conspicuous, disbanded to melt into the interior. Its various members dispersed to various centers of Red influence, and it was Mao's bad luck that the member who first showed up in Kiangsi (disguised as a Catholic priest) was senior to him in the party hierarchy, a younger but very assertive and influential man named Chou En-lai. Chou wasted no time in countermanding much of what Mao had established not only in military tactics but also in civilian matters like land reform. This was in September, the month in which Japan took Manchuria.

The threat of Japanese conquest of China alarmed Mao more than The Flying General ever had. In January 1932, after the Japanese attack on Shanghai, he anxiously proposed that the party offer to join forces with Chiang and everyone else interested in resisting the Japanese. In April he even persuaded the Kiangsi provincial government to declare war on Japan. But in none of this did he receive any support from the national party leaders. Since Moscow was not interested in resisting Japan, the Twenty-Eight Bolsheviks were not interested, and therefore the party was not interested—especially in joining forces with fascists like Chiang.

Mao might well have expected that any suggestion from him, whatever the party's ideological mind-set, was likely to be ignored, since he had been officially consigned to the outer darkness at a party conference held early in November 1931. Dominated by the Twenty-Eight, the conference had passed a resolution viciously attacking Mao's policies, both military and civilian. He was accused of opportunism, pragmatism, empiricism, and deficiency in ideological fervor. (On another occasion, because he advocated tactical retreats, he was even accused of "flightism"!) The Japanese threat was ignored, flexible guerrilla tactics were replaced with military concepts of frontal engagements, and any agrarian revolution was declared subject to the leadership of the industrial proletariat.

But later that month, at the more broadly representative First All-China Soviet Congress, Mao's supporters rallied—after all, Mao had founded the party a decade earlier and was hardly friendless—and the Twenty-Eight found themselves stymied. Mao was elected to head the Central Executive Committee of the All-China Soviet Government and reelected as chief political commissar of the First Front Army in Kiangsi. In addition, several of his friends were elected commissars to governmental departments. The net result was a stalemate, with Mao generally in control of the Red shadow government, including the military, and his opponents in control of the party. The latter, with Moscow's encouragement, did manage to inveigle the Congress into passing resolutions reflecting the ideological positions and programs of the Twenty-Eight.

Despite the stalemate, Mao's control of the government left him in an inferior position, since under Communism the party is supreme. This became clear during 1932 in Kiangsi, where his position in the party was subordinate to that of Chou En-lai. Chou opposed Mao's guerrilla tactics as too inconclusive, preferring the more tangible outcomes of direct confrontations. Early that year the First Front Army's failure to take the important city of Kanchow strengthened his position, although the failure may have been due more to his meddling than to the tactics used. By August he managed, with ardent support from the Twenty-Eight, to take over the control of the entire Red Army. Over the next year and a half Mao's position and influence, political and military, would be eroded into impotence.

When Chiang Kai-shek carried his fourth "encirclement and annihilation" campaign into Kiansi in the winter of 1932–1933, several of Mao's more stubborn supporters among the Red Army commanders refused to employ Chou's confrontation tactics, using instead Mao's style of mobile maneuver. Although Chiang's attack was once again thwarted, Chou, thoroughly irritated, took over

Mao's post as political commissar of the First Front Army. Meanwhile his supporters busily employed pen and tongue to condemn Mao's "rightism," especially his administration of land reform, regarding which he was considered too soft on small landlords.

In January 1933 he was expelled from the Politburo and replaced by one of the Twenty-Eight. During that year he endured an uneasy symbiosis with his adversaries, who would have liked to send him on a missionary expedition to the North Pole but hesitated to take any drastic action against him because of his broad popular following. In fact, he was at first mildly pleased when, in January 1934, at the Second All-China Soviet Congress, he was reelected chairman of the Soviet Government. But it soon became clear that he was merely a titled supernumerary. The majority held by the Twenty-Eight Bolsheviks on the quasi-legislative Presidium gave them the power simply to dismiss him. Rather than do anything so conspicuous, however, in February they jostled him out of the presidency of the Council of People's Commissars and then incited his successor into promulgating a decree censuring him for mismanagement of the land reform program.

Meanwhile Chiang had mobilized nearly a million troops for a fifth "encirclement and annihilation" campaign. Over Mao's futile protests the Red Army chose to meet the first assault more or less head-on, despite the enemy's vastly superior numbers and consequent advantage in any sort of confrontation. The Red defeat was a disastrous one, but still his voice remained only a cry from the encircling gloom. As the alarm in the party hierarchy grew over a rapidly deteriorating predicament—not only were Chiang's troops generally having a field day at the Red Army's expense, but the Japanese had defeated a Chinese force *south* of the Great Wall— Mao suddenly found himself in the role of scapegoat. On the grounds, again, that he had committed military and agricultural errors of great consequence, he was barred from all party gatherings and formally disgraced. His situation was serious, even personally threatening, at least enough for him to go into hiding. In August he was found and put under house arrest, and immediately came down with malaria. (He had a reputation for psychosomatic, and often convenient, illnesses.) One day a friend, bringing him some wine and chicken, found him in a state of reminiscing depression. As the two men talked over the early days of their comradeship in the party, Mao sounded thoroughly defeated, lamenting the disappearance of so much that they had struggled for.

By early October the party pooh-bahs had become so frantically alarmed by Chiang's relentless advances that they invited Mao to a meeting with Chou En-lai and other leaders to discuss strategy. The strategy decided on was wholesale retreat from the Kiangsi province. The end of the month saw the beginning of the Long March. And in January 1935, some 400 miles to the west, a special meeting of the available party leaders was called at which Chou confessed to an embarrassing number of serious mistakes and declared himself converted to Mao's views. His influence was enough to bring most of the others into line, and Mao was elected chairman of the newly formed Revolutionary Military Council and restored to his military leadership. As this juncture, of course, with the Communists in headlong flight to an uncertain destination, this was something like being elected captain of the *Titanic* with decks already awash.

The Long March began with about 100,000 men in Kiangsi and ended with about 5,000 in Shenshi. In between were 370 days of forced travel, including 270 days and 6,000 miles of walking through country ranging from the barely passable to the virtually impassable—over eighteen mountain ranges (five of them perpetually snow-covered), across twenty-four rivers (many torrential), and through six areas occupied by hostile aborigines. All along the way the weary marchers were harassed by Chiang's ground troops and strafed by his planes. By comparison, an eighteenth-century trip from southern Tennessee, through Texas and New Mexico, then north through the Colorado Rockies and then back east to Lake Michigan (analogous to the route of the Long March) would have been a lark. By the end of this ordeal Mao was so firmly in the military and political saddle that there would never again be a serious effort to unseat him.

# George Gershwin and *Porgy and Bess*

During the early 1920s in Charleston, South Carolina, a severely crippled beggar became something of a celebrity. Black as coal except for the gray in his hair, he wandered about the street ensconced in a small box mounted on wheels and pulled by a goat. Born Samuel Smalls, he was known everywhere as "Goat Sammy." His condition was pitiable, and alms-inspiring, but he also may have been the meanest man in town. His handicap by no means rendered him either helpless or gentle. He had a lengthy, colorful police record of violent physical assaults, mostly against women. His last recorded assault was an abortive attempt to shoot a woman, for which he was arrested and jailed. Before the trial, however, he disappeared from the jail, and later a body identified as his was discovered in a shallow grave on a nearby coastal island.

The newspaper account of his character and his final days greatly impressed DuBose Heyward, a Charleston resident, whose novel *Porgy* was published in 1925. Porgy's deformity and goat cart were the same as Sammy's, but his behavior was not nearly as unsavory. Although capable occasionally of cunning malice, or a malicious cunning, he was a very sympathetic character whose tragic heroism helped to make the book a huge success. In the fall of 1927, the book, rewritten and somewhat softened for the stage by Heyward and his wife, was produced by the Theater Guild in New York, received much praise, and ran for a very profitable twelve months.

George Gershwin read the novel in 1926 and immediately began thinking of it in terms of a musical drama. He wrote Heyward at once and soon thereafter met with him in Atlantic City to discuss collaborating on a musical version of the story. But both men were busy at the time with other commitments and could agree on nothing more definite than getting together again someday. When Gershwin saw the play in 1927, he became more determined than ever to write the opera—just as soon as he could finish up all these other things....

Five years later, in March 1932, he again wrote Heyward, and in reply Heyward again expressed great interest in the project. But the best that the harried Gershwin could come up with, as a starting date for their collaboration, was January 1933. Heyward waited until September 1933, when he called Gershwin to report that the Theater Guild wanted his permission to produce a musical based on *Porgy*, to be written by Jerome Kern and Oscar Hammerstein II and to star Al Jolson. Although he had been caught in one of the 1933 bank failures and was short of cash, Heyward assured Gershwin that he was reluctant to see *Porgy* translated into a musical comedy; he would much prefer to see it as a folk opera, the sort of thing that he and Gershwin had discussed. On the other hand, a musical with Jolson in it would undoubtedly bring him a lot of money. But if you'll start on the opera soon, he told Gershwin, I'll say no to the Guild. Impressed, Gershwin promised to get started without further delay. Heyward said his no to the Guild, the Kern-Hammerstein-Jolson trio withdrew, and Gershwin started keeping his promise. He probably did not realize that he had promised two years of his life to Heyward.

At the outset the collaborators found themselves faced with a practical problem. Heyward could not leave Charleston and Gershwin could not leave New York. Their solution was to invite Ira Gershwin to join them in the collaboration. Since he was not tied down, he could act as liaison, and since he was a brilliant lyricist, he could, and did, make a substantial contribution to the work (such as "It Ain't Necessarily So"). By October that work was far enough along for George to be offered a bonus of $5,000 for signing a contract with the Metropolitan Opera. He declined, fearing that the Met might give the opera three or four performances in its first year and perhaps fewer, if any, in subsequent years. He felt that a folk opera should be seen by as many folks as possible. That same month he signed with the Theater Guild.

The next two years may have been the most intensive work period in his live. After a couple of brief visits with Heyward in December, he returned to spend several weeks in the summer of 1934 to soak up the Charleston atmosphere, visiting homes, churches, and miscellaneous gathering places in black neighborhoods, listening intently to the conversations and especially to the singing. He became thoroughly absorbed in the operation—as Heyward was to write later, "to George, it was more like a homecoming than an exploration." During July and August the partners in creation worked in a simple shack on a small harbor island about ten miles from town, where they paid a high price for their quiet isolation in the form of suffocating heat and a rich variety of voracious flying insects.

During the fall and winter Heyward and the two Gershwins worked feverishly to shape up the story line and give it musical life. The tunes kept tumbling out of George's piano—"Summertime," "I Got Plenty o' Nuthin'," "Bess, You Is My Woman Now," "It Ain't Necessarily So"—while the words poured out of his lyricists' pens. By mid-April the manuscript was close enough to completion to permit plans for opening in the fall. Rouben Mamoulian, who had directed the stage play, agreed to direct the opera. He and the Gershwins spent the summer in busy preparation, revising the book, selecting the cast, creating the sets, orchestrating the music, and, early in September, starting rehearsals. George found the first rehearsal thrilling, even though it went rather badly. The music sounded so marvelous to him, he told Mamoulian with an appealing mixture of vanity and modesty, that he couldn't believe he wrote it. Everyone seemed to share his excitement and his confidence that *Porgy and Bess* would be a tremendous hit.

Problems cropped up by the gross during rehearsals. Since the work was a trailblazer, many of the problems were unprecedented. The role of Sportin' Life, for example, was given to John W. Bubbles, a splendid tap dancer with years of experience on the vaudeville circuit. But he could not read music and, although his voice quality was satisfactory, his singing was alarmingly innocent of proper pitch, tempo, or rhythm. The slow triplets in "It Ain't Necessarily So" were quite beyond him. Gershwin was ready to give up, but Mamoulian persevered, and when the singing coach, Alexander Steinert, came up with the brilliant idea of tap dancing the rhythms out for Bubbles, the ground was laid for a memorable characterization. Problems also abounded in cutting the opera down to size from its four-and-a-half-hour length. (Even if this length was not too much for an audience, Gershwin conceded, it would be too much for the singers).

The opera opened in Boston on September 30, 1935, with many a musical celebrity in the audience—Cole Porter, Irving Berlin, Serge Koussevitzky, Sigmund Spaeth. The response was one of unalloyed enthusiasm not only from the audience but also from the Boston critics. The Gershwin entourage began looking forward eagerly to taking New York by storm. And indeed, when it opened there on October 10, the audience reaction was as gratifying as it had been in Boston.

But the reviews were mixed, at best. Although the drama critics' comments were generally favorable, those of the music critics—to which George was naturally more sensitive—were anything but. Olin Downes found the work rather unresourceful and shallow, and was uncomfortable with its vacillation from opera to operetta to musical comedy and back again. Lawrence Gilman wrote that the opera's songs were weak, catered to popular taste, and constituted "blemishes upon its musical integrity." The duet between Porgy and Bess ("Bess, You Is My Woman Now") he dismissed as "rubbish." Virgil Thomson branded the opera as a "fake" and, like Downes, seemed uncomfortable with its failure to fit neatly into a respectable pigeonhole: "It is crooked folklore and halfway opera, a strong but crippled work... falsely conceived and rather clumsily executed." Similarly, Samuel Chotzinoff, ordinarily a Gershwin fan, complained that as "entertainment it is hybrid, fluctuating constantly between music drama, musical comedy, and operetta." Paul Rosenfeld condemned it for failing to sustain a mood.

Even more discouraging were reactions from black musicians and critics. The music critic Ralph Matthews described the score as unsatisfying, lacking in the "jubilee spirit" and "the deep soul-stirring songs" of his race, and denounced it for its "conservatory twang." Hall Johnson considered the work itself "stiff and artificial," though rescued partly in performance by a superlative black cast. And Duke Ellington announced that it was imperative "to debunk Gershwin's lampblack Negroisms." Or, as Johnson had put it, the work was "an opera about Negroes rather than a Negro opera."

The criticism took its toll at the box office, despite a long reply from Gershwin published in the October 20 New York Times. The opera ran to dwindling houses for 124 performances (compared to the play's 367), losing money all the way. It continued in this vein after January 1936, when it hit the road for a three-month tour. It did make history at the end of the tour, in Washington, D.C., but not in the conventional way. For the first time in a century, the audience at the National Theater was not segregated.

George Gershwin never again saw his opera performed. In January 1942, four and a half years after his death, Cheryl Crawford introduced New York to a shorter, tighter, more swiftly paced Porgy and Bess. This time, the music having become much more familiar through record sales, the response from public and critics alike was overwhelmingly favorable. The production played on Broadway for eight months, to full houses, and then went on a long and hugely successful tour—after which it returned to New York for another run. It had become a very lucrative enterprise indeed, and one of the most satisfying aspects of this revival was that a good portion of the profits went to an investor in the Crawford gamble named Rose Gershwin, George and Ira's mother.

# Lucille Ball and the Bottom Rungs

She was too tall. She was too thin. She couldn't act. She couldn't dance. She had no stage presence. She moved awkwardly. Training her for any of the performing arts, the director of her drama school had advised her devoted mother, was just a waste of good money.

But Lucille Ball was determined, even stubborn—more so than most fifteen-year-olds, and indeed more so than the vast majority of adults in show business. Whatever the things might have been that she could *not* do, she could outwork most beavers, even eager ones. Further, there was something in her character that suppressed such feelings as envy, rancor, malice. Although she might experience such emotions on occasion, she quickly learned never to cultivate them or let them distract her attention from the next rung up on the show biz ladder.

But those first ten years or so—from about 1927 to 1937—were bleak enough to discourage Pollyanna's sunnier sister. Commuting irregularly from her home in upper New York State to the Great White Way (staying with friends while in the Big Apple), she developed a talent for picking herself up after being knocked down. The knock-downs, and put-downs, were all too frequent. At Earl Carroll's, showcase for the well-rounded figure flecked with rhinestones, she was fired after only two weeks of rehearsal. She picked herself up and tried out at Ziegfeld's. Chosen for a job in the chorus of *Rio Rita,* she threw herself into several weeks of unpaid rehearsals only to be told by the stage manager to go home and forget about show business. And so on.

Her sideline jobs as soda jerk, store clerk, whatever, barely kept her afloat. At times she was really flat broke, without even a nickel for a cup of coffee. This was true enough for her to remember later a technique she followed for survival. In a cafe she would watch a customer order coffee and doughnuts. Often he would eat one of the two doughnuts, drink the coffee, and depart, leaving behind a nickel tip. Lucy would hop onto his stool, order another cup of coffee, pay for it with his nickel, and have the second doughnut with her precious java. There also were some transportation problems. One evening she found herself at the subway station with only four cents. The fare was five cents, so she "panhandled for a penny," as she described it later. One man she approached offered her ten dollars, but she refused. She managed to get home without getting into that kind of show business.

This unremitting struggle, laced with frequent rejections from show-biz authority figures, was a depressing experience even for someone as buoyant as Lucy. There were times when it got too much for her and she thought of ending it, and her life along with it. She considered throwing herself in front of a car—in Central Park, where the traffic was heavy, fast, and lethal. But when she was in these fatalistic moods, she discovered, she always seemed to add a modifying touch. She would prefer, for example, that the fateful car making its way through Central Park be a limousine driven by a chauffeur and owned by a young, handsome, unattached man in the rear seat. Such modifications, she felt, meant that she wouldn't end it all today. Maybe tomorrow.

Life became a little easier when she got a job modeling coats in the garment district. Coats had the advantage, she believed, of hiding her "missing figure." But then a fellow model offered her a job with her husband, a commercial photographer. Perhaps her face and figure were improving, for she was soon being offered jobs to model clothes in modish department stores and even to pose for commercial artists and photographers. A job at Hattie Carnegie's brought in $35 a week in addition to her other, less regular income.

But she paid a price for her newfound affluence. After all those months of malnutrition, she could not keep up the frantic pace without ruining her health. At Carnegie's one day she suddenly collapsed with stabbing pains in her legs and abdomen. Rushed to a doctor, she was told that she was suffering from severe fatigue, brought on by her eating, and noneating, indiscretions. And from acute rheumatoid arthritis. A long rest was imperative, she was advised, together with traction therapy and a radical change in her eating habits. Although the advice was anything but welcome, she took it and went home. She managed to stay away from New York for two years. And she definitely changed her eating habits. She would never again try to live on coffee and doughnuts, however scant her resources.

Hattie Carnegie rehired her on her return to New York. With her health restored, Lucy looked better than ever before, and soon she was also doing better as a model than she ever had before. In the background, however, show business still beckoned, and in the summer of 1933 the beckoning became irresistible when a New York agent told her of a job opening as a "poster girl" in an upcoming Goldwyn movie. She had appeared in a billboard campaign for Chesterfield cigarettes, and Hollywood was interested. Would she be willing to go to California? Would she ever!

Hattie Carnegie encouraged her to take a flyer, giving her some clothes and promising her that she could have her modeling job back if things didn't work out. Within a week or so Lucy was in Hollywood and under contract to the Goldwyn studios. Although she couldn't know it yet, she had exchanged her early period of outright rejection for a period of benign neglect. It was a fair exchange but no bargain.

As those of us who enjoy watching familiar faces in old movies can attest, Hollywood in the early thirties was largely a collection of established repertory companies tied by contract to the various studios and dominated by the star system and fanatic cults of personality. Moviegoers of the time also enjoyed seeing familiar faces on the screen, and the studios catered to this demand by showing them familiar faces as often as possible. The newcomer was an unknown comer, if a comer at all. It was a typical Catch-22 situation. You had to get your face on the screen often enough to make it familiar to audiences, but you weren't likely to because it wasn't familiar enough to audiences. Lucy's reputation as a Broadway performer was hardly spectacular enough to break this vicious circle.

These were the days when names like Beery and Dressler, Cooper and Garbo, Gable and Shearer, Huston and Crawford, Fields and West were lighting up marquees all over the country. Not names like Lucille Ball. But then Lucy wasn't doing so bad. She was a Goldwyn Girl, selected by none other than Busby Berkeley, who was later to make the Hollywood musical a thing apart. She was pulling down $150 a week in times when $25 was a respectable salary and a quarter of the nation's workers had no salary at all. But the movies she played in during the year and a half she worked for Goldwyn (four for Goldwyn and six on loan to other studios) were generally dogs, and in none of them was she given any billing. She was becoming a little more familiar now as a face on the screen, but as a pretty face without a name.

Disheartened by such anonymity, she asked to be released from her contract. Goldwyn agreed amiably, expressing his regret that things hadn't worked out. Lucy quickly signed with Columbia for half the Goldwyn salary but with some hope that she could break out of the chorus and the showgirl stereotype. And she did, but not in a very promising direction. Since Columbia at the time was a B-picture factory, she found herself working as an extra and in bit parts in comedy shorts that consisted mostly of being frantically pursued by The Three Stooges. But in a 1935 turkey entitled

*Carnival* she was assigned a minor part, as a nurse. And for this, her nineteenth film, she finally was given the billing that she so desperately wanted.

It did her little good, however. Shortly thereafter the studio went on an economy kick, her option was dropped, and she was looking for work again. She found it, at RKO, but at the price of another reduction in income. She was making only a dismaying third of what she had been two years earlier at Goldwyn's. And she was back in the showgirl pigeonhole. In her first RKO movie, *Roberta,* her role consisted of walking down a staircase dressed in an elaborate costume. For this performance she was given plenty of ostrich feathers but no billing.

Yet her performance evidently impressed somebody, for she was put under contract and enrolled in RKO's talent school. Here she received genuine dramatic training from Ginger Rogers's mother, Lela, working on a genuine stage before a genuine audience. She found it exhilarating. It also may have helped her to a speaking part (one line) in a flower shop scene in the Astaire-Rogers classic movie *Top Hat.* And then to a larger part, with billing, in a film starring the Metropolitan Opera's Lily Pons and an up-and-coming young man who would later become a good friend of Lucy's, Henry Fonda.

But the part was only larger, not large. For the next couple of years Lucy slaved away in the Hollywood cellar, earning ever more money but nonetheless relegated to miniscule bit parts in rare blockbusters and to somewhat larger roles in turkeys. She felt thoroughly stymied. Then she was offered the lead role in a musical comedy on the stage, *Hey Diddle Diddle,* which was scheduled to open in Princeton, New Jersey, and from there to go eventually on to Broadway. It did open, in January 1937. But the male lead, Conway Tearle, died in February, and the play closed. Lucy returned disconsolately to RKO, knowing that her defection had done nothing to enhance her position at the studio.

Yet soon after her return she landed a part in *Stage Door,* which, as a movie about aspiring actresses living in a theatrical boarding house, offered an unusually large number of female roles. With Ginger Rogers and Katharine Hepburn in the leads, the studio reached down much lower on the ladder for three supporting roles. The three hopefuls selected were Eve Arden, Andrea Leeds and Lucille Ball. The other four women constituted pretty fast company, histrionically, but Lucy triumphantly held her own. RKO renegotiated her contract with a gratifying raise, and began giving her better roles. Her performances brought her an offer to join a popular radio show as a comedienne. The part gave her an opportunity to display her comedic talent, and she was a tremendous success.

It was only the beginning, of course. Waiting for her along the road ahead was a magic box called television, with a Cuban singer in it.

# Richard Rodgers
# and *Oklahoma!*

In 1923 Richard Rodgers was a thoroughly frustrated man. He and lyricist Lorenz Hart had written a musical comedy based on the famous story of the poet Francois Villon and entitled *If I Were King*. Rodgers thought it was very good. He found a producer or two who thought it was at least pretty good. But he could not find anyone who would risk any money on it. He was sharply reminded that he was only twenty-one and Hart was only twenty-six, and you could hardly expect anyone to have much confidence in artists so young and inexperienced. (As an amateur production the show inspired a Broadway impresario to back a Rudolf Friml version a couple of years later. It was the smash operetta entitled *The Vagabond King*.)

Rodgers could not deny his age but he resented the charge of inexperience. He had written dozens of scores for musical comedies. Of course, they had been amateur productions, mostly during his student days at Columbia College and the Institute of Musical Art, yet they had brought him no little acclaim. He had done very respectable work at the Institute, which was New York's most reputable school of music. He had been musical director for a Shubert Brothers touring vaudeville company. And he had shared

196

composing credits with Sigmund Romberg three years earlier for a
moderately successful Broadway musical, *Poor Little Ritz Girl*. He
was in that old Catch-22 bind—how can you get experience if
everyone rejects you because you haven't had enough experience?

An opportunity arose when he heard that a certain producer was
looking for material for a new show. Rodgers and Hart had created
a musical called *Winkle Town* some years before but had never
been able to sell it. Rogers took it to the producer, who said the
songs were acceptable, perhaps, but not the book. This gave
Rodgers the idea of offering him the songs without the book—
camel's nose strategy, he hoped. The producer, doubtful, asked
Rodgers if he would be willing to play the songs for a friend, Max
Dreyfus, a music publisher of towering reputation. Rodgers
agreed. After the audition Dreyfus told the producer that the
music was worthless and that he really ought to look up Vincent
Youmans. Rodgers was too flabbergasted to be angry.

Desperately, he and Hart then tried another ploy. Since full-
fledged musical comedies were so expensive to produce, they
wrote a play about an old Austrian-born composer reduced to
writing arrangements for Tin Pan Alley tunes. Given the subject,
they could not resist writing a couple of songs; how they managed
to resist writing several dozen more remains a mystery, but the fact
testifies to their determination. Determination, however, was not
enough. Although Hart's father inveigled a thousand dollars of
backing from Billy Rose, a sufficient boost to get it launched on
Broadway, it closed after an embarrassingly short run. Despite the
fine performance of a young actor named Fredric March in the
lead, the critics' thumbs were turned uniformly down. One of the
thumbs was that of George Jean Nathan, who wrote that the plot
was bad enough to ruin any play, "even Hamlet." Rodgers and
Hart vowed never again to try sneaking up on Broadway with some
pale imitation of a musical comedy.

In his memoirs fifty years later Rodgers described the winter of
1924–1925 as the "most miserable period of my life. No matter
what I did or where I turned, I was getting nowhere." Day after

depressing day he made the rounds of publishers' and producers' offices with his sheaf of songs, with rejection congealing into dejection. Failure was especially hard to put up with because things were *not* tough all over. As he made his gloomy rounds he could see continual evidence of other people's smash hits: Rudolf Friml's *Rose Marie*, Sigmund Romberg's *The Student Prince*, George Gershwin's *Lady, Be Good!*, Irving Berlin's *Music Box Revue*, and another elaborate *Ziegfeld Follies*. And when he got home he could read about the accolades with which Vincent Youmans's *No, No, Nanette* was being showered in Chicago. He could also nurse his feelings of guilt over his parasitical dependence on his parents at a time when his brother was slaving away at medical school. He was so despondent that he did not touch a piano for weeks.

That was not the depth of his despondency. The time had come, he decided, to get a respectable job for a self-respectable outlook. A friend told him that he knew a businessman who wanted to retire and was seeking someone to take over his business. It was a small business—indeed, *he* was it, a wholesaler in infants' wear. It would mean that Rodgers would be responsible for all the buying and selling, as well as all the considerable traveling. The work would certainly keep him busy, perhaps even busy enough to keep his mind off Broadway and environs. And the starting salary during the training period would be $50 a week, which was $50 a week more than Rodgers's current earned income.

He impressed the man at the interview and was offered the job. Suddenly he was seized by sober second thoughts. Not without some embarrassment, he asked if he could sleep on it and give his answer in the morning. His would-be employer, although somewhat puzzled since they had hit it off splendidly, agreed. Rodgers went home in a state of nervous uncertainty.

That evening a friend of his father's called him, a theatrical lawyer who had shown a good deal of interest in his work and who indeed had persuaded his father that the son should be allowed to follow his own bent. Some young people, Benjamin Kaye told him, most of them bit players for the Theater Guild, were planning a benefit show. They needed a songwriter, and Kaye had persuaded them that he knew just the man. Rodgers thanked him but said that he had decided not to work on any more amateur productions and was in fact giving up any thought of a musical career. He had been offered a job, and he was going to grab it. Kaye assured him that it was his decision, of course, but that Theresa Helburn and Lawrence Langner would be disappointed.

The names made a great difference to Rodgers. The discussion continued. Helburn and Langner were the guiding spirits of the Junior Players for the Theater Guild, and said players wanted to show their appreciation of that solicitous guidance by putting on a revue that might bring in some money to buy tapestries for the Guild's new 52nd Street Theater. So this would be something more than an amateur show. It would display professional, if young, talent, would be sponsored by the Guild, and would be pretty sure to attract not only a full house but also many influential producers and critics. It would run for only one day (matinee and evening), but Rodgers became more and more convinced that this one day could make all the difference in the world to him. That morning he turned down the infants' wear job.

Immediately problems arose. One of the prospective leads in the show was an actress with literary talents, and it had been understood that she would write all the lyrics. It had never occurred to Rodgers that he would be working with anyone but Larry Hart, and now he risked his stake in the show by insisting that Hart would have to do the lyrics. Luckily, the actress was not all that interested in a career as lyricist, and once again the old team was in harness.

Another problem, unexpectedly, was Hart. He was not all that impressed with the Guild's sponsorship and was very reluctant to make another investment of time and creative energy for a return of bitter disappointment. Rodgers cajoled, pleaded, compromised, haggled, and finally succeeded in persuading his partner to give it One More Try. Once they had started working together again,

Hart's reluctance dissolved. There's no business like show business for stimulating the inspiration glands.

The two performances were given at the Garrick Theater on Sunday, May 27, 1925, and at both the audiences reacted with an uproarious standing ovation lasting through ten curtain calls. The next day Rodgers arranged for repeat performances over the next several weeks, at times when the theater was not otherwise occupied. These performances met with similar enthusiasm from the audiences and, as the critics grew aware that there was a new hit in town, began earning rave notices. Before long, The Garrick Gaieties took over the theater full time, running twenty-five weeks for a hundred and sixty-one performances. And the Guild's new tapestries were downright gorgeous.

Some years later, when their careers were in full flower, the two collaborators attended a show at the Guild's theater and commented on the tapestries. "We're responsible for them," said Hart. "No," Rodgers answered, "they're responsible for us."

A delayed aftermath of the Guild tapestry production was the musical *Oklahoma!*, which was a failure over several months in one sense, yet only momentarily in another.

In 1942 the Theater Guild, having run a gauntlet of box office flops, was broke. Helburn and Langner had a prescription for financial recovery: a Rodgers and Hart musical revue. They had just the book for it, too: Lynn Riggs's play, *Green Grow the Lilacs*, which the Guild had produced eleven years earlier. Rodgers had read the script at their request and, enchanted by the play's southwestern rural charm, eagerly agreed to write the score. But Larry Hart, it turned out, was in no condition to write the lyrics. Sodden from the compulsive drinking that had developed into a chronic illness, he insisted to Rodgers that he had to go to Mexico to dry out. Rodgers, countering that they both knew that the trip to Mexico would simply be another drinking spree, offered to hole up with his friend in a sanatarium, where they could work on *Lilacs* together. Hart refused; he *had* to go to Mexico. Rodgers warned that *he* had to have a lyricist for the *Lilacs* show, if not Hart, then someone else. Was he thinking of anyone in particular? Yes, Oscar Hammerstein. You couldn't find anyone better, said Hart— adding, however, the first negative comment of the many that the show proposal was to receive. He simply did not think that the play could be turned into a good musical revue. And then he went to Mexico, to return in even worse shape. He died in 1943, of pneumonia.

Rodgers and Hammerstein got along delightfully right from the beginning, partly because Rodgers—unlike Friml, Kern, Romberg, or Youmans before him—was willing in general to compose his music to Hammerstein's words, rather than the other way around, and partly because Hammerstein's prodigious talent could furnish finished lyrics within a time when one might have expected no more than an idea in embryo. Almost immediately they agreed on a director, Rouben Mamoulian, whom they had both worked with earlier, though separately. Helburn and Langner, however, perhaps because Mamoulian had directed the Gershwins' great *Porgy and Bess* in the financially disastrous 1935 version, resisted on the grounds that Mamoulian, with his Russian background, could not do well with a story about the American southwest. But Rodgers and Hammerstein's total agreement on the selection proved irresistible. Whatever tension this may have created apparently evaporated when the writing team enthusiastically adopted Helburn's recommendation for dance director, the young but promising choreographer Agnes De Mille.

Creating the show had its problems, but *the* problem arose after creation. Like creation itself in the Garden of Eden, it proved impossible to sell in New York. Rodgers and Hammerstein, together with the leads, Alfred Drake and Joan Roberts, endlessly made the rounds of penthouse parties, reading script and singing songs in wearying efforts to convert the thoroughly sauced guests into angels. They were about as successful as an alms collector for a temperance union would have been.

The show, first entitled *Away We Go!* and then, with misgivings,

*Oklahoma!*, simply had too many strikes against it. *Green Grow the Lilacs* had failed at the box office. Mamoulian's only other experience in directing a Broadway musical was with the 1935 *Porgy and Bess,* another box office flop. Hammerstein had been associated with nothing but financial turkeys on Broadway for the past ten years. And Rodgers, although he had been doing just fine with Larry Hart, was an unknown quantity (or quality) now that he was working with another lyricist. Beyond the people involved, there was the revue itself, offering folk ballet in place of popular chorus girl dancing, a viciously unpleasant character (Jud Fry), and even violence and murder. The production included no stars, no big names (Howard da Silva, Celeste Holm, Joan McCracken, Bambi Lynn were then virtual unknowns). If you need $83,000 to put on this show, the Guild people were told, you'd better go look for it elsewhere.

They did so. Helburn went to M-G-M (which had long before bought the Guild's rights to *Green Grow the Lilacs*) and offered half of any *Oklahoma!* profits for $75,000 and the movie rights for another $75,000. Although in a sense the second amount covered the first, it was no deal. Well, since you have so little confidence in the show, replied Helburn, how about giving us an option to buy back the rights to *Lilacs* after the musical opens in New York? This M-G-M consented to do, provided that the Guild bought back the rights within thirty days after the opening. Although the Guild did so, hastily, within thirty hours after the opening and thereby eventually reaped a goodly sum, the agreement netted Helburn exactly zilch at the moment when she so desperately need the rough and ready cash.

When a Broadway producer told Harry Cohn, president of Columbia Pictures, about the difficulties in raising money for the show, Cohn promised backing from Columbia if Rodgers and Hammerstein would agree to write the screenplay. But not even he was able to convince Columbia's board of directors to put up a cent, red or otherwise. Cohn then invested $15,000 of his own, a gesture of confidence that at least helped to bring quite a few smaller angels on board.

Eventually the $83,000 was amassed from scores of small contributions—charitable contributions seemed to be what most of the givers considered their investments—and the show opened first in New Haven and then in Boston in March 1943. Although the audiences reacted favorably, scouts from Broadway sent back a chorus of negative reports adding up to "It'll never make it in the big time." A gag about it made the rounds: "No legs, no gags, no *chance!*"

Nevertheless it opened at the end of the month in New York. The house was not sold out for that first night—the first and last time for the next several years—although the audience's enthusiasm grew steadily during the performance, culminating in a deafening ovation at the final curtain. But the verdict of the critics had yet to be heard, and the writers, producers, and principals gathered to await it at a party in a sponsor's home. At midnight they gathered around a radio to listen to a drama critic whose program was widely considered a reliable early sample of the anxiously anticipated notices. He reported that the show wouldn't run for more than a few performances. Everyone sagged.

A few hours later, however, as the morning newspapers began hitting the streets with their reviews, it became clear that *Oklahoma!* was not merely a hit. It was a sensation.

# Sidney Poitier and the American Negro Theater

"Dear President Roosevelt," the young man just out of the army wrote haltingly, laboriously, "I am from the Bahamas. I would like to go back to the Bahamas but I don't have the money. I would like to borrow from you $100....I will send it back to you and I would certainly appreciate it very much. Your fellow American, Sidney Poitier." Thirty-five years later Poitier would write in his autobiography, "Never heard from the cat."

And so he did not go back to the Bahamas, for all his intense yearning. He spent the winter of 1944–1945 in New York, and by spring, after he had turned eighteen, he was convinced that he would never see that hundred dollars. But with the aid of the help wanted ads in the local *Amsterdam News*, he managed to earn subsistence money from the mountains of dishes always waiting to be washed in hundreds of restaurant kitchens. One day, while looking through the want ads, he happened to notice a small headline on an adjacent page: "Actors Wanted by Little Theater Group." It aroused his curiosity, since he had no idea of what actors did but suspected that it probably was easier than washing dishes.

A day or so later, when he went to the address given in the article, he found the American Negro Theater in the basement of a library. The door was opened by a man who introduced himself as the director. He invited Poitier in.

An actor, eh? — Yes, sir! — Ever acted before? — Oh, yeah! — Where? — Lots of places, Florida, Nassau. — Okay, you take this script and go up on the stage and read John's part starting on page twenty-seven.

But Poitier had never been on a stage, had never even seen one, did not know what a script was or what it was for, barely knew how to read anything weightier than a help wanted ad, and spoke with a soft, singsong Caribbean accent virtually unintelligible anyplace north of Miami. He "read" one line and was escorted firmly from the theater with the advice to take up dishwashing. As he walked dejectedly away, a row of dirty dishes sixty years long stretched out before him. The thought of it was unbearable. There had to be another way to get through this life. Like being an actor. But how in the world—?

One thing was sure: The accent had to go. Most of it, anyway. He had to be easily understood by theatergoers, who were mostly average white Americans with an accent like Harry Truman's. He would have to listen to them closely and constantly, but how? They might not like his dogging their footsteps with cupped ears. Then a light went on inside, and with his earnings from his next batch of dishes he bought a small radio. Over the next six months he listened to that radio every free waking moment. Everything— sports, drama, news, even commercials and station identifications. After six months of this, instead of losing his mind, he was clearly on his way to losing his accent, or at least that large part of it that made him unintelligible to potential audiences.

When he was not listening to the radio during those six intensive months he was reading, especially during breaks and slow times at work. At one restaurant one of the waiters spent untold hours helping him to read the *New York Journal-American*, acting as his dictionary. Poitier's account of his relationship with this gentle Jew graces his autobiography in touching terms: "This soft-spoken, natural teacher, with thick bifocals, bushy eyebrows, and silver-white hair, sat with me night after night in the twilight of his years and gave me a little piece of himself.... I have never been able to thank him properly because I never knew then what an enormous contribution he was making to my life. I don't know if he's alive or dead, probably dead by now, but he was wonderful, and a little bit of him is in everything I do."

At the end of six months Poitier felt that he was ready for another go at the American Negro Theater. He found it at a new address, where it had a bigger theater and stage and better classrooms. He asked for the director, who wasn't there, but he was told when to come in for the next auditions. When he arrived some days later he joined about seventy-five other hopefuls who, he noticed uneasily, were mostly reading, or mumbling lines from, *plays*. All that he had brought with him was a copy of the magazine *True Confessions*, from which he had memorized a couple of paragraphs. When his turn came, the drama coach listened patiently but briefly to the true confession and then asked if he would be willing to do an improvisation. He agreed eagerly, although he had not the least idea of what an improvisation might be. But with a few words of instruction he caught on quickly. Suppose you're in the jungle, she told him, a soldier in combat—now think about it a few minutes and let us know when you're ready. He thought about it, despairingly, and then gave an imitation of Jimmy Cagney spraying machine gun bullets into the imaginary shrubbery. This seemed to go well enough but, when he decided to fall with an enemy bullet in his midsection, he remembered that he had worn his only good clothes to this audition and was about to ruin them on a dirty floor. So he held out one arm and supported his stiff body on that arm and his feet in a salient and successful effort to keep off the floor. It was not a very convincing death. All right, thank you, said the drama coach, and we'll let you know if we need you.

About a week later an astonishing postal card arrived in his mail asking him to come into the theater for a talk. He did, and was asked if he would be willing to join the company on a three-month trial basis, even though there wasn't much hope for him. What he did not know was that forty of the hopefuls on that afternoon of auditions had passed their tests, but all were girls. So about a dozen men had to be dredged out of the rejects, and Poitier, it turned out, was at the bottom of *that* group. But he was delighted—until he discovered that his accent was still strong enough to invite derision during the training sessions. And although he kept on trying, he was told at the end of the three months that he really had not shown any noticeable improvement. He was wasting his time and the faculty's, and it would be best if he would quietly go away.

Desperately, he asked for another chance, for more time. No. For a week he wandered catatonically amid his dishes until another light went on. He returned to the theater and offered to take over all the janitorial duties from the students, who were pretty careless about them, if he could continue with the training. The faculty gave the proposition some sympathetic thought, and he had a deal. To find a job with regular hours that he could accommodate to the theater's schedule, he hunted about in the garment district and found one in a blouse factory (owned by a man named Abzug who had a daughter-in-law named Bella—*the* Bella). The new schedule worked out fine.

He was well into his second trial period when a part came up that made his mouth water—a character named Liebman in a play entitled, *Days of Our Youth*. But the coach brought in an outsider named Harry Belafonte for the role. When Poitier's fellow aspirant players protested in his behalf, the coach compromised by making him Belafonte's understudy. And sure enough, at a rehearsal one evening Belafonte failed to show up and Poitier played the part. The drama coach had invited James Light, a Broadway director, to see the rehearsal, after which Light asked Poitier to drop by his office the following Monday. Poitier was afraid that his performance must have been bad enough to invite some more advice about returning to the dishwashing game.

Instead, that Monday he was offered the small part of Polydorus in Gilbert Seldes's version of *Lysistrata*, the Greek comedy, which Light was planning to produce with a cast of blacks. He snatched it up hungrily, of course, and, after joining Actors' Equity, felt very professional indeed. His rehearsals for the play he remembers as "the best four weeks of my life," but on opening night, after seeing the audience of some 1,200 people, he froze in terror. Shoved out on the stage, he stared out at the audience with glazed eyes ("Mama," he cried inwardly, "what am I doing here?"), and then came out with his third line instead of his first. The other actor in the scene responded with the line that was supposed to follow Poitier's first line, to which Poitier responded by saying his seventh line. By this time the hesitations and confusions had the audience, who had been pretty glum up to this point, in merry if disconcerting stitches. Poitier and his desperate colleague continued—the colleague tried line three, Poitier responded with line twelve, and so on. The audience, delighted, began applauding. Somehow Poitier managed to get through all his lines and leave the stage with as much dignity as utter humiliation would allow. He fled the theater without waiting for curtain calls and the traditional party.

After "the most agonizing night of my life," he pored through the thirteen reviews in the morning papers. All panned the play mercilessly, but a few praised the new actor playing Polydorus for bringing (as one put it) an "acute comedic approach" to the part. The problem was that he could not possibly repeat that performance, and on the next three nights he did a much more conventional and less interesting job. On the last of those nights the play closed.

But on opening night John Wildberg had been in the audience. Wildberg was the producer of *Anna Lucasta*, then a major Broadway hit. He intended to put the show on the road—would Poitier, he asked over the phone, be interested in joining the company as an understudy? Poitier tried to say yes without bringing a new comedic approach to telephone communication. On the road he learned several parts well enough to fill in, which he did for the first time one evening in Philadelphia. This time the butterflies did not turn into icicles and immobilize him. In fact, things went very well throughout the long, invigorating tour.

He returned to New York in 1949 and applied for a role in the forthcoming Kurt Weill musical *Lost in the Stars*. But Hollywood intervened in the form of the director Joseph L. Mankiewicz, who, after some auditioning, offered him a film part at ten times the salary he would have received for the musical. The movie, *No Way Out*, was a memorable debut that led to another major role in the film of *Cry the Beloved Country* and on to an Academy Award for his performance in *Lilies of the Field* in 1963.

# Thomas Bradley and the Los Angeles Woodwork

In Los Angeles in 1969, *Newsweek* reported, "with the May 27 runoff elections only days away, it appears all but certain that Tom Bradley, the son of a Pullman porter, will dethrone wily Sam Yorty and become the first Negro mayor of the nation's third-largest city."

There was good reason to think so. Thomas Bradley, fifty-one, six-foot-four and pleasantly dignified, was an attractive candidate running against a mercurial and less dignified incumbent who had garnered only 26 percent of the vote in the nonpartisan primary a month earlier (to Bradley's 42 percent, in a field of thirteen candidates). Bradley was also a man of independence and determination. Advised by adults against going to college after his graduation from high school in 1937, he nonetheless attended the University of California at Los Angeles on an athletic scholarship and, during his subsequent twenty years on the Los Angeles police force, attended two other universities to earn a law degree.

In 1961 Lieutenant Bradley, discouraged by the racial odds against further promotion, retired from the force to set up a private law practice.

The jump from law into politics is a traditional one. Two years later he ran for the city council from his district, the Tenth, which was about a third black, a third white, and a third "other." He won, becoming the first black ever elected to the council. His first four years as councilman impressed the district's voters enough for them to reelect him in 1967.

But he was not the only vote-getter in town. Sam Yorty had completed his first four years as mayor in 1965, and he also had impressed enough voters to get himself elected to a second term. In that second term, however, he seemed to grow too big for his mayoral britches, indulging in more than a dozen world tours, during which he entertained the media with controversial comments on international relations, including such strident and unwavering support of U.S. actions in Vietnam that he came to be known, at least among his critics, as "Saigon Sam." In 1968, although theoretically a Democrat, he had refused to back Hubert Humphrey against Richard Nixon. And perhaps because of his work absences, three of his appointees were convicted of accepting bribes. His posturing as a colorful maverick seemed to attract extremists from both ends of the political spectrum, but support was draining fast from the large area in between.

Meanwhile Bradley was drawing increasing support from just that area, including an active organization of some 10,000 volunteer workers. Since the city was only about one-sixth black, his campaign deemphasized his color—selectively. His picture, for example, did not appear in his newspaper and television ads, although in the black sections of town it was displayed on posters and in community papers, often showing him with the late Martin Luther King, Jr., and sound trucks toured those neighborhoods advising the residents that "Bradley is beautiful!" His publicity campaign was a vigorous one, as indeed it had to be. Despite his six years on the council—or perhaps because of them, since the reward for working in any kind of committee environment is usually anonymity—public opinion polls had revealed that he was known by name to only 7 percent of the voters at the start of the primary campaign.

On the morning after his primary victory Bradley was accused of conducting a "racist campaign" by a surprised and bitter Yorty. "I didn't run telling people to vote for me because I'm white. He ran around telling people to vote for him because he was Negro." Although Bradley's chief appeal had been for "a coalition of conscience" that included blacks, Hispanics, and liberal white Democrats, Republicans, and independents, Yorty evidently decided that his predicament called for a racial-radical approach in the runoff campaign. A Bradley victory, he warned a suburban Rotary luncheon group, would be an invitation to black militants to converge on city hall and intimidate the council—and would the police dare to arrest these friends and supporters of the mayor? He inveighed darkly against outsiders trying to influence the election, politicians like Senator Edward Kennedy, who had had it up to here with Sam Yorty—although Yorty's fulminations were directed more against other, more mysterious outsiders such as "left-wing radicals and, if you please, identified Communists." Bradley, he asserted, was supported by none other than Gus Hall, America's Number One Communist. This last may have been true, at least in the sense that Hall was not very likely to support Yorty. Bradley's comment on the charge was simply a reference to Ronald Reagan's riposte in his 1966 gubernatorial campaign: "When people support me, they're buying my philosophy—I'm not buying theirs." Bradley was nothing but a Communist front, Yorty insisted, in a Red experiment for taking over a large U.S. city. In white areas of the city leaflets appeared in mailboxes slyly urging the residents to vote for Thomas Bradley and thereby "make Los Angeles a black city." A Yorty ad depicted Bradley in a rather formidable pose and asked, "Will your family be safe?" And posters bombarded citizens with the thoughtful slogan, "America — Love It or Leave It."

Tactics like this surely lost Yorty some votes in the center. On one occasion, before a thoroughly middle-class white audience, he brought up the Gus Hall association and received a goodly round of boos and catcalls. But the tactics were very effective in calling out of the woodwork a great number of nervous, naive citizens whose sole interest in the election was to prevent Los Angeles from being taken over by such as the Black Panthers. Since the city was, after all, still suffering from reverberations of the terrible Watts riots of 1965, as well as more recent uprisings, the opportunities for cheap shots were many and, for Yorty, irresistible. Bradley's rather stolid campaign, on the other hand, concentrated on local issues that at times seemed almost irrelevant amid the swirling charges of Red perils and Black threats.

And so Bradley's campaign was a failure. Yorty's tactics, which Bradley later described as the dirtiest in the city's history, were simply too much for him. Of the city's 1,100,000 eligible voters, 840,000, or 75 percent, turned out to give Yorty a third term with a 53 percent majority. And perhaps significantly, in the school board election two moderate incumbents were replaced by two newcomers who had concurred in Yorty's identification of the issues.

Four years later, in 1973, the adversaries staged a rerun. "Travelin' Sam" had resumed his junketeering in his second term, spending an accumulated total of more than a year away from his job. Watergate had replaced Watts as a major concern among voters, and a story that some of Yorty's aides had bought him a paid-up life insurance policy for $50,000 taken from campaign contributions helped their man not at all. This time, in addition, Bradley started off at a recognition level not of 7 percent, but of 95 percent. And this time Yorty's scare tactics had less effect on the woodwork. Bradley was elected with 56 percent of the vote. And reelected in 1977. And again in 1981, 1985, and 1989.

# Ronald Reagan and the 1976 Convention

Ten years after the Goldwater debacle of 1964 the American political pendulum had begun swinging the other way, slowly and tentatively but (at least in hindsight) unmistakably. Lyndon Johnson's Great Society programs were still flourishing, but his (and his successors') failure to put either those programs or the Vietnam War on a pay-as-you-go basis had been generating a growing anxiety in the body politic. Could the federal government continue living on credit along with an ever-increasing burden of debt? Was it financially resilient enough to protect the country's economy from the inflationary threat of OPEC oil price increases? Was it growing so big and so unwieldy as to be suffocating? Nervous questions like these cried out for a simple answer, such as Ronald Reagan's favorite, "Deficit spending is responsible for all the economic problems confronting us today."

And so in the summer of 1974, during his eighth and last year as governor of California, several of his friends and political colleagues began meeting to discuss his prospects as a presidential candidate in 1976. By early 1975, with Richard Nixon self-destructed and replaced by a lackluster Gerald Ford, those prospects were looking brighter every day. Ford obviously was going to be another "me-too" candidate whose unbalanced budgets would be harbingers of four more years of fiscal irresponsibility. And so Reagan people—Michael Deaver, John Sears, Lyn Nofziger, and others—commissioned some opinion polls, which revealed enough support to give their man a solid fighting chance to win the nomination and even the election.

His radio program, which had an audience of between 10 and 15 million listeners, mostly rapt, and his syndicated column, appearing in some 180 newspapers, had kept him somewhat in the public eye, and this public image maintenance could be readily augmented by stepping up the rubber chicken circuit riding and exploiting opportunities for media coverage.

They were encouraged that others, even rivals, also considered Reagan a strong potential candidate. As early as December 1974 they were heartened by a phone call from Ford to Reagan concerning some deflective job openings for him at the cabinet level, and by similar approaches when Reagan visited Washington the following spring. As the weeks flew by, the pressure on Reagan grew. To some extent he was being challenged by the right wing ideologues to put up or shut up. He had been articulating their views, and his, for the past ten years, and here was a chance to *do* something about the situation. Was he a man or a mouse? In November 1975 he gave the only possible answer.

During the first half of 1976 the battle of the primaries resounded across the land, seesawing vigorously but never wildly enough to unseat either Ford or Reagan. By mid-July, a month before convention time, the delegate counters were calling it a horse race, with Ford being given the benefit of any edge. The Reagan camp, worried about that edge, decided to counter Ford's liberal-conservative, all-things-to-all-ideologies tactics with a similar ploy of their own. If Reagan could be persuaded to break precedent and announce his choice of running mate *before* the balloting for the presidential nomination, Ford might thereby be forced to do likewise. If he chose a liberal, he would alienate some conservatives, and vice versa. He would be bound to lose some support.

But then, curiously, the Reagan people dropped into their own trap. They fell victim to the conventional practice (in both senses of "conventional") of "balancing" a ticket. A nice balance for their conservative western governor would be a liberal—but moderately liberal, you understand—eastern Senator. In this connection Reagan's reflector in the Senate, Paul Laxalt of Nevada, recommended his senatorial seatmate, Richard Schweiker of Pennsylvania. Hastily, perhaps. As he explained later, there was a lot of anxiety that the media might at any moment declare that Ford had the 1,130 votes needed to win, and then the uncommitted delegates could turn from Reagan for good. The crucial area of decision was the northeast—New York, New Jersey, Pennsylvania—and Schweiker ought to be a natural for keeping it at least undecided.

Laxalt had a high opinion of Schweiker's intelligence and character, but his opinion of his political coloration differed from the consensus. Schweiker was generally considered one of the most liberal Republicans in the Senate, partly because of early (and later regretted) votes for social welfare programs. Unlike Reagan's ex-liberalism, Schweiker's had not had time to sink into hard conservative heads, especially since his current stands on most social issues were still well to the left of Czar Nicholas and therefore, at best, suspect. If Reagan & Co. had asked Congressional conservatives for advice, they would have learned what a load of eggs they were about to throw into the fan. Instead, they asked Schweiker to fly to California for an audition and, after he had passed, simply notified various Washington conservatives. Senator Jesse Helms of North Carolina, for instance, who had been a fervent Reaganite, later remembered the precise time of his telephone call, 9:05 P.M., because it brought him the greatest shock of his life. Congressman Phil Crane of Illinois was stunned,

Congressman Bill Brock of Tennessee thought it was some kind of fraud, and others were sure that a practical joker was at work. Congressman Gene Snyder of Kentucky, who believed the report, remarked that Reagan had "sold his last cow to buy a milking machine." And Senator John Ashbrook of Ohio branded the selection as "the dumbest thing I've ever heard of," adding, "You can't trust any of them."

But apostasies were expected to be outweighed by conversions. Schweiker's own Pennsylvania surely could be counted on for a generous portion of its 103 votes, if not most of them. After Pennsylvania had thus led the way, other northeastern states' delegations would follow suit. But the chairman of the Pennsylvania delegation had promised Ford 90 votes, including his own, and nothing Schweiker could say in their grueling four-hour telephone call could budge him from that promise. Without Pennsylvania, no significant switches could now be expected in other delegations. As this dismal situation unfolded—the price in conservatives already paid but without any liberal deliveries—the Reagan forces learned that Jesse Helms and some like-minded colleagues were promoting Senator James Buckley of New York as a dark horse candidate for the Presidential nomination. They found Buckley's ideological proximity to the Czar far more acceptable than Schweiker's sinister remoteness, of course, but Helms's explanation to the Reagan team was that Buckley could probably draw enough of the uncertain support from both sides to prevent a majority for either side on the first ballot. Then the delegates committed to Ford on the first ballot could switch to Reagan on the second.

Evidently Ford & Co. agreed with this scenario, anxiously. Appropriate pressure was exerted on Buckley by New York party heavyweights. Buckley tactfully withdrew with a public statement that there simply had not been "enough time to mobilize potential support in an effective and resourceful way.'

Meanwhile the Reagan group had prepared a new "Rule 16-C" and were pushing for its adoption by the convention. It required each candidate for the presidential nomination to name a running mate before the balloting began. But this effort to recoup the Schweiker losses was voted down by the convention—although narrowly, 1,180 to 1,069. Schweiker offered to withdraw, but Reagan would not hear of it.

Ford won the nomination on the first ballot. The conventional wisdom (again in both senses of "conventional") was that this was Ronald Reagan's swan song, his last hurrah. He would now lose much of his political base. The party could boast many young "neoconservatives" eager to replace him. After all, in the 1980 election year he would be sixty-nine years old. In other words, politically dead.

# Bibliography

**Moses and His Temper**

Exodus: 2–4

Cook, F.C. (ed.). *The Bible Commentary*. Grand Rapids, Michigan: Baker Book House, 1975.

*Good News Bible*. New York: American Bible Society, 1976.

Knox, Ronald. *The Old Testatment in English*. New York: Sheed & Ward, 1948.

Stack, Hagen. *Living Personalities in the Old Testament*. New York: Harper & Row, 1964

Wiesel, Elie. *Messengers of God*. New York: Random House, 1976

**Cleopatra and the Gabinians**

Bradford, Ernie. *Cleopatra*. New York: Harcourt Brace Jovanovich, 1971

Grant, Michael. *Cleopatra*. London: Weidenfeld & Nicolson, 1972.

Lindsay, Jack, *Cleopatra*. New York: Coward, McCann & Geoghegan, 1970.

Ludwig, Emil. *Cleopatra: The Story of a Queen*. New York: Viking Press, 1937

**Jesus and the Establishment**

Baldwin, Louis. *Jesus of Galilee*. Valley Forge, Pennsylvania, 1979.

219

Buttrick, George Arthur, *et al. The Interpreter's Bible*. Nashville: Abingdon-Cokesbury Press, 1951.

*Good News Bible*. New York: American Bible Society, 1976

Grispino, Joseph S. *The New Testatment of the Holy Bible* Confraternity Version). New York: Guild Press, 1966.

Kleist, James A., and Joseph L. Lilly (trs.). *The New Testament*. Encino, California: Bruce Publishing Co., 1956.

Ludwig, Emil. *Son of Man*. New York: Liveright Publishing Co., 1945.

Phillips, J.B. (tr.). *The Gospels*. New York: Macmillan Publishing Co., 1953.

## Muhammad and the Quraish of Mecca

Andrae, Tor. *Mohammed: The Man and His Faith*. New York: Harper & Row, 1977.

Glubb, John Bagot. *The Life and Times of Muhammad*. New York: Stein & Day, 1970.

Rodinson, Maxime. *Mohammed*. New York: Pantheon Books, 1971.

Watt, W. Montgomery. *Muhammad, Prophet and Statesman*. New York: Oxford University Press, 1974.

## Alfred the Great and the Battle of Chippenham

Bryant, Arthur. *Makers of England*. Garden City, New York: Doubleday & Co., 1962.

Churchill, Winston S. *History of the English-Speaking Peoples*. New York: Dodd, Mead & Co., 1965.

Helm, Peter J. *Alfred the Great*. New York: Thomas Y. Crowell Co., 1965.

Loyn, H.R. *The Vikings in Britain*. New York: St. Martin's Press, 1977.

Mapp, Alf J. *The Golden Dragon*. LaSalle, Illinois: Open Court, 1974.

## Galileo and the Inquisition

Broderick, James, S.J. *Galileo: The Man, His Work, His Misfortunes*. New York: Harper & Row, 1964.

Christianson, Gale E. *This Wild Abyss*. New York: Macmillan Co., 1978, pp. 249–309.

Ley, Willy. *Watchers of the Sky*. New York: J.B. Lippincott Co., 1964, pp. 105–32.

Rogers, Frances. *5000 Years of Stargazing*. New York: J.B. Lippincott Co., 1964, pp. 65–73.

Ronan, Carl A. *Galileo*. New York: G.P. Putnam's Sons, 1974.

*Science News*, November 1, 1980, p. 77.

Thiel, Rudolph. *And There Was Light*. New York: Alfred A. Knopf, 1957, pp. 138–63.

## George Washington and Fort Necessity

Emery, Noemie. *Washington: A Biography*. New York: G.P. Putnam's Sons, 1976.

Fleming, Thomas J. (ed.). *Affectionately Yours, George Washington*. New York: W.W. Norton & Co., 1967.

Flexner, James T. *George Washington*. Boston: Little, Brown & Co., 1965.

Freeman, Douglas S. *George Washington: A Biography*. New York: Kelley Publishers, 1975 (1948 ed.).

Knollenberg, Bernhard. *George Washington: The Virginia Period*. Durham, North Carolina: Duke University Press, 1964.

Marshall, John. *Life of George Washington*. New York: AMS Press, 1969

Sears, Louis M. *George Washington*. New York: Thomas Y. Crowell Co., 1932.

## Napoleon Bonaparte and the Fall of Robespierre

Castelot, André. *Napoleon*. New York: Harper & Row, 1971.

Cronin, Vincent. *Napoleon*. London: William Collins, 1971.

Fouriner, August. *Napoleon I: A Biography*. London: Longmans, Green, 1911.

Ludwig, Emil. *Napoleon*. New York: Liveright Publishing Corp., 1926.

Rose, John. *The Life of Napoleon I*. New York: Macmillan Co., 1902.

## Simón Bolívar and Puerto Cabello

Masur, Gerhard. *Simón Bolívar*. Albuquerque: University of New Mexico Press, 1969.

O'Leary, Daniel F. *Bolívar and the War of Independence*. Austin, Texas: University of Texas Press, 1970.

Sherwell, Guillermo. *Simón Bolívar*. Clinton, Massachusetts: Colonial Press, 1921.

Whitridge, Arnold. *Simón Bolívar, the Great Liberator*. New York: Random House, 1954.


### Gioacchino Rossini and *The Barber of Seville*

Harding, James. *Rossini*. New York: Thomas Y. Crowell Co., 1971.

Stendahl. *Life of Rossini*. Seattle: University of Washington Press, 1972 (1824 ed.).

Toye, Francis. *Rossini: A Study in Tragi-Comedy*. New York: W. W. Norton Co., 1963.

Weinstock, Herbert. *Rosini: A Biography*. New York: Alfred A. Knopf, 1968.


### Samuel F. B. Morse and the Telegraph

Larkin, Oliver W. *Samuel F. B. Morse and the American Democratic Art*. Boston: Little, Brown & Co., 1954.

Mabee, Carleton. *The American Leonardo*. New York: Octagon Books, 1969.

Prime, Samuel. *The Life of Samuel F. B. Morse*. New York: D. Appleton, 1875.


### Mary Godwin and *Frankenstein*

Dunne, Jane. *Moon in Ecliple: A Life of Mary Shelley*. London: Weidenfeld & Nicolson, 1978.

Florescu, Radu. *In Search of Frankenstein*. Boston: New York Graphic Society, 1975.

Gerson, Noel B. *Daughter of Earth and Water*. New York: William Morrow & Co., 1973.

Glut, Donald F. *The Frankenstein Legend*. Metuchen, New Jersey: The Scarecrow Press, 1973.

Grylls, R. Glynn. *Mary Shelley*. New York: Haskell House, 1969.

Nitchie, Elizabeth. *Mary Shelley*. New Brunswick, New Jersey: Rutgers University Press, 1953.

## Walt Whitman and *Leaves of Grass*

Allen, Gay Wilson. *The Solitary Singer*. New York: New York University Press, 1955.

Canby, Henry Seidel. *Walt Whitman, an American*. Boston: Houghton Mifflin Co., 1943.

Kaplan, Justin. *Walt Whitman*. New York: Simon & Schuster, 1980.

Kouwenhoven, John (ed.). *Leaves of Grass and Selected Prose by Walt Whitman*. New York: The Modern Library, 1950.

Rupp, Richard (ed.). *Critics on Whitman*. Coral Gables, Florida: University of Miami Press, 1972.

Trimble, W.H. *Walt Whitman and Leaves of Grass*. Folcroft, Pennsylvania: Folcroft Library Editions, 1905.

## Abraham Lincoln and the Election of 1858

Benson, Godfrey Rathbone (Lord Charnwood). *Abraham Lincoln*. New York: Henry Holt, 1916.

Luthin, Reinhard B. *The Real Abraham Lincoln*. Englewood Cliffs, New Jersey: Prentice-Hall, 1960.

Nicolay, John G., and John Hay. *Abraham Lincoln: A History*. New York: Century Co., 1904.

Sandburg, Carl. *Abraham Lincoln*. New York: Harcourt, Brace & Co., 1926.

Thomas, Benjamin. *Abraham Lincoln*. New York: Alfred A. Knopf, 1962.

## Ulysses S. Grant and Civilian Life

Catton, Bruce. *U.S. Grant and the American Military Tradition*. Boston: Little, Brown & Co., 1954.

Lewis, Lloyd. *Captain Sam Grant*. Boston: Little, Brown & Co., 1950.

McFeely, William S. *Grant: A Biography*. New York: W.W. Norton, 1981.

## Fyodor Dostoevsky and the Roulette Tables

Carr, Edward H. *Dostoevsky: A New Biography*. Folcroft, Pennsylvania: Folcroft Library Editions, 1977 (1931 ed.).

Lloyd, J.A.T. *Fyodor Dostoevsky*. New York: Charles Scribner's Sons, 1947.

Mackiewicz, Stanislaw. *Dostoyevsky*. London: Orbis, 1947.

Mochulsky, Konstantin. *Dostoevsky: His Life and Work*. Princeton, New Jersey: Princeton University Press, 1971.

### Paul Cézanne and the Fogies

Mack, Gerstle. *Paul Cézanne*. New York: Alfred A. Knopf, 1936.

Rewald, John. *Paul Cézanne: A Biography*. New York: Simon & Schuster, 1948.

Schapiro, Meyer. *Cézanne.* New York: Harry N. Abrams, 1952.

Vollard, Ambrose. *Paul Cézanne: His Life and Art*. New York: N.L. Brown, 1923.

### Georges Bizet and *Carmen*

Cooper, Martin. *Georges Bizet*. Westport, Connecticut: Greenwood Press, 1971.

Curtis, Mina. *Bizet and His World*. New York: Alfred A. Knopf, 1958.

Dean, Winston. *Bizet*. London: J. M. Dent, 1948.

Parker, Douglas C. *Bizet: His Life and Works*. New York: Arno Press, 1926.

### Mohandas Gandhi and the Practice of Law

Fisher, Louis. *Gandhi: His Life and Message for the World*. New York: New American Library, 1954.

Gandhi, Mohandas K. *Gandhi: An Autobiography*. Boston: Beacon Press, 1957.

Mehta, Ved. *Mahatma Gandhi and His Apostles*. New York: Viking Press, 1977.

Sheean, Vincent. *Lead, Kindly Light*. New York: Random House, 1949.

### Thomas Edison and the "Ogden Baby"

Conot, Robert. *A Streak of Luck*. New York: Seaview Books, 1979.

Josephson, Matthew. *Edison: A Biography*. New York: McGraw-Hill, 1959.

Kaufman, Marvyn D. *Thomas Alva Edison.* New York: Dell Publishing Co., 1968.

## Sigmund Freud and the "Dream Book"

Clark, Ronald W. *Freud: The Man and His Cause.* New York: Random House, 1980.

Freud, Sigmund. *The Origins of Psychoanalysis.* New York: Basic Books, 1954.

Natenberg, Maurice. *The Case History of Sigmund Freud.* Chicago: Regent House, 1980.

Puner, Helen W. *Freud: His Life and His Mind.* New York: Grosset & Dunlap, 1947.

## The Wright Brothers and Sales Resistance

Combs, Harry. *Kill Devil Hill.* Boston: Houghton Mifflin Co., 1979.

Reynolds, Quentin. *The Wright Bothers.* New York: Random House, 1950.

Walsh, John E. *One Day at Kitty Hawk.* New York: Thomas Y. Crowell, 1975.

## Pablo Picasso and *Les Demoiselles d'Avignon*

Broeck, William. *Picasso.* New York: Harry N. Abrams, 1955.

Cabanne, Pierre. *Pablo Picasso: His Life and Times.* New York: Willian Morrow & Co., 1977.

Kozloff, Max. *Cubism/Futurism.* New York: Charterhouse, 1973.

Penrose, Roland. *Picasso: His Life and Work.* Berkeley: University of California Press, 1981.

Raboff, Ernest. *Pablo Picasso.* New York: Doubleday & Co., 1968.

## Eugene O'Neill and the Bottle

Carpenter, Frederic I. *Eugene O'Neill.* New York: Twayne Publishers, 1964.

Gelb, Arthur and Barbara. *O'Neill.* New York: Harper & Row, 1962.

Miller, Jordan L. *Playwright's Progress: O'Neill and the Critics.* New York: Scott, Foresman Co., 1965.

Schaeffer, Louis. *O'Neill, Son and Artist.* Boston: Little, Brown & Co., 1973.

## Winston Churchill and Gallipoli

Baldwin, Hanson W. *World War I: An Outline History.* New York: Harper & Row, 1962.

Carter, Violet Bonham. *Winston Churchill: An Intimate Portrait.* New York: Harcourt, Brace & World, 1965.

Churchill, Winston S. *The World Crisis.* New York: Charles Scribner's Sons, 1949.

Costigan, Giovanni. *Makers of Modern England.* New York: Macmillan Co., 1967.

Falls, Cyril. *The Great War.* New York: Capricorn Books, 1959.

Fishman, Jack. *My Darling Clementine: The Story of Lady Churchill.* New York: New American Library, 1971.

Martin, Ralph G. Jennie: *The Life of Lady Randolph Churchill.* New York: New American Library, 1971.

Moorehead, Alan. *Gallipoli.* New York: Harper & Bros., 1956.

Pelling, Henry. *Winston Churchill.* New York: E.P. Dutton & Co., 1974.

Taylor, A.J.P., Basil Liddell Hart, et al. *Churchill Revised: A Critical Assessment.* New York: Dial Press, 1969.

Taylor, Robert Lewis. *Winston Churchill: An Informal Study of Greatness.* New York: Doubleday & Co., 1962.

## Harry Truman and the Haberdashery

Daniels, Jonathan. *The Man of Independence.* New York: J.B. Lippinccott Co., 1950.

Hayman, Leroy. *Harry S. Truman.* New York: Thomas Y. Crowell Co., 1969.

Robbins, Jhan. *Bess and Harry.* New York: G.P. Putnam's Sons, 1980.

Steinberg, Alfred. *The Man from Missouri.* New York: G.P. Putnam's Sons, 1962.

## Walt Disney and the Distributors

Schickel, Richard. *The Disney Version.* New York: Simon & Schuster, 1968.

Thomas, Bob. *Walt Disney.* New York: Simon & Schuster, 1976.

Montgomery, Elizabeth R. *Walt Disney.* Westport, Connecticut: Garrard Publishing Co., 1971.

Walker, Greta. *Walt Disney*. New York: G.P. Putnam's Sons, 1977.

## Cole Porter and *See America First*

Ewen, David. *Popular American Composers*. New York: H.W. Wilson Co., 1962.

Hubler, Richard G. *The Cole Porter Story*. New York: World, 1965.

Schwartz, Charles. *Cole Porter: A Biography*. New York: Da Capo Press, 1979.

## Billy Mitchell and the Wild Blue Yonder

Burlingame, Roger. *General Billy Mitchell: Champion of Air Defense*. New York: McGraw-Hill Book Co., 1952.

Hurley, Alfred F. *Billy Mitchell: Crusader for Air Power*. New York: Franklin Watts, 1964.

Mitchell, Ruth. *My Brother Bill*. New York: Harcourt, Brace & Co., 1953.

## Clark Gable and His Broadway Doldrums

Jordan, Rene. *Clark Gable*. New York: Pyramid Publications, 1973.

Tornabene, Lyn. *Long Live the King*. New York: G.P. Putnam's Sons, 1976.

Williams, Chester. *Gable*. New York: Fleet Press, 1968.

## Laurence Olivier and *Journey's End*

Cottrell, John. *Laurence Olivier*. London: Weidenfeld & Nicolson, 1975.

Daniels, Robert L. *Laurence Olivier: Theater and Cinema*. London: Tantivy Press, 1980.

Hirsch, Foster. *Laurence Olivier*. Boston: Twayne Publishers, 1979.

## Humphrey Bogart and the Wood Splinter

Benchley, Nathaniel. *Humphrey Bogart*. London: Hutchinson Publishing Group, 1975.

Hyams, Joe. *Bogie*. New York: New American Library, 1967.

McCarty, Clifford. *Bogey*. Secaucus, New Jersey: Citadel Press, 1965.

Michael, Paul. *Humphrey Bogart: The Man and His Films.* Indianapolis: Bobbs-Merrill Co., 1965.

## Mao Tse-tung and the Twenty-Eight Bolsheviks

Howard, Roger. *Mao Tse-tung and the Chinese People.* New York: Monthly Review Press, 1977.

Suyin, Han. *The Morning Deluge: Mao Tse-tung and the Chinese Revolution.* Boston: Little, Brown & Co., 1972.

Uhalley, Stephen, Jr. *Mao Tse-tung: A Critical Biography.* New York: New Viewpoints, 1975.

Wilson, Dick. *Mao, The People's Emperor.* London: Hutchinson Publishing Group, 1975.

## George Gershwin and *Porgy and Bess*

Ewen, David. *George Gershwin: His Journey to Greatness.* Westport, Connecticut: Greenwood Press, 1970.

Rushmore, Robert. *Life of George Gershwin.* New York: Macmillan Co., 1968.

Schwartz, Charles. *Gershwin: His Life and Times.* New York: Bobbs-Merrill Co., 1973.

## Lucille Ball and the Bottom Rungs

Gregory, James. *The Lucille Ball Story.* New York: New American Library, 1974.

Morella, Joe, and Edward Epstein. *Lucy, The Bittersweet Life of Lucille Ball.* Secaucus, New Jersey: Lyle Stuart, 1973.

Parish, James R. *The RKO Gals.* New Rochelle, New York: Arlington House, 1974.

## Richard Rogers and *Oklahoma!*

Ewen, David. *Richard Rodgers.* New York: Henry Holt, 1957.

Green, Stanley. *The Rodgers and Hammerstein Story.* New York: Da Capo Press, 1980.

Rodgers, Richard. *Musical Stages: An Autobiography.* New York: Random House, 1975.

## Sidney Poitier and the American Negro Theater

Ewers, Carolyn. *Long Journey: A Biography of Sidney Poitier.* New York: New American Library, 1969.

Paige, David. *Sidney Poitier*. Minneapolis: Creative Education, 1977.

Poitier, Sidney. *This Life*. New York: Alfred A. Knopf, 1980.

## Thomas Bradley and the Los Angeles Woodwork

*New York Times Magazine*, February 24, 1974, pp. 16+.

*Newsweek*, April 14, 1969, pp 36–37; May 26, 1969, pp. 40+; June 11, 1973, pp. 29–30.

*Time*, April 23, 1969, p. 26; June 6, 1969, pp 28–29; June 11, 1973, pp 17–18.

## Ronald Reagan and the 1976 Convention

Boyarsky, Bill. *Ronald Reagan*. New York: Random House, 1981.

Drew, Elizabeth. *American Journal: The Events of 1976*. New York: Random House, 1977.

Edwards, Lee. *Ronald Reagan: A Political Biography*. Woodside, New York: Nordland Publishing Co., 1981.

Smith, Hedrick. *Reagan: The Man, the President*. New York: Macmillan Co., 1981.

Van der Linden, Frank. *The Real Reagan*. New York: William Morrow & Co., 1981.